THE STORY OF
Father Dominique Pire

THE STORY OF

Father Dominique Pire

WINNER OF THE NOBEL
PEACE PRIZE

AS TOLD TO
Hugues Vehenne

Translated from the French by
JOHN L. SKEFFINGTON

New York
E. P. DUTTON & CO., INC.
1961

First published in the U.S.A., 1961
by E. P. Dutton & Co., Inc.

English Translation Copyright, ©, 1960
by E. P. Dutton & Co., Inc., New York,
and Hutchinson & Co. (Publishers) Ltd., London
All rights reserved. Printed in the U.S.A.

FIRST EDITION

Published in England under the title of EUROPE OF THE
HEART and in Brussels, (Belgium) as SOUVENIRS &
ENTRETIENS, du R. P. Dominique Pire.

Library of Congress Catalog Card Number: 60-9747

CONTENTS

PHOTOGRAPHS

(In one section of twelve pages following page 64)

1. The Pire family: Father, Mother and the children.
   Little Georges is at his father's right

   Georges Pire in 1928, before he entered the monastery

   Brother Dominique as a student in Rome

2. At the time of celebrating his first Mass, at Dinant,
   July, 1937

   1944: Chaplain in the "Secret Army" of the Resistance

3. The D.P. camps: ancient barracks and human distress

4. Aerial view of the European Village at Bregenz, Austria

5. Father Pire holding Ceslaw Averon, first child born in the
   first European village, at Aix-la-Chapelle

   The European Village at Aix-la-Chapelle

6. The Nansen European Village at Berchem-Sainte-
   Agathe, near Brussels

   Father Pire laying the first stone of the Anne Frank
   European Village, 31st May, 1959

7. "He will be able to dream in peace"

8. Father Pire at the window of his little office at Huy

9. Father Pire at work in his office on the Rue du Marché,
   at Huy

MAP

FOREWORD

———————————•———————————

THE WISE MEN OF NORWAY awarded the Nobel Peace
Prize for 1958 to a Belgian Dominican, the Reverend Father
Dominique Pire, for his ten years of labour in the cause of
his fellow men.

A whole human forest had been laid waste in the tem-
pests which had buffeted Europe during and after the
Second World War, and at the centre of the cyclone in
Austria and Germany millions of refugees, the Displaced
Persons or D.P.s, were whirled about like logs in a mael-
strom of human misery.

When the Nations came forward to divide these uprooted people among them, they put their wealth, skill,
and practical turn of mind to devising a splendid contrap-
tion for sifting through these unfortunates. One poured
dollars in one end and healthy and happy emigrants came
out at the other—a good, saleable commodity.

The sieved-out residue, the Hard Core—the weak, the
old, the invalid, the sick—was left behind: Europe's
human surplus for whom there was no market.

These were the people Father Pire wanted to put back
on their feet. He was trying to replant the forest.

The Nobel Prize was awarded to him on three counts.
Firstly, because this Catholic priest had come to the aid of
these unfortunate people, and carried them in his arms,
without looking back to see if their souls were following.
Secondly, because his work had been the spontaneously
and disinterestedly heroic endeavour of a single man, who

had acted with as much disregard for racial, political, and national barriers as for sectarian ones. He had given a silent demonstration that there were problems which officialdom's bureaucratic methods either could not, or would not, solve. Finally, because the example of his work had brought men closer together, in that people here and there the world over had combined to help the suffering by giving their labour, extending their heart-felt sympathy, and contributing funds. In this way, the suffering which once served to separate mankind, now served to unite them.

It was this third reason which was decisive in ensuring the award of the Nobel Peace Prize to Father Pire.

It has made no difference in him. He still has his passionate love of truth, his fiery independence, and still keeps in front of him the same goal, the brotherhood of men.

I have watched him in action and heard him speak. It is to me that he has told the story of his life and his work, and one can see in this book how the two first mingle and then become indistinguishably one—a single river.

I present it to the reader in all sincerity, and in the hope that the account may serve a useful purpose. If it be true that the world is passing from the era of Charity to that of Social Security, from patriarchal mutual aid to the Destitution-Relief Machine, it is still a good thing that a few lonely men should fight a heroic rearguard action.

May they remain as shining beacons to show later generations that all joint human action needs, not merely organization, health regulations, and justice in its execution, but a spirit of fraternal loving kindness.

Father Pire is among these lonely souls. He keeps guard and devotes his fame in all its purity to reminding this age of the high dignity of those who are unfortunate.

HUGUES VEHENNE

THE STORY OF
Father Dominique Pire

CHAPTER ONE

A Prayer—in order that
I may be Understood

DEAR LORD,

In the midst of my way along the road of life—if it be Thy will to keep me here on earth for some while to come—I have told my story to a friend. I told it to his heart, not merely dictated it to his pen, and took him genuinely into my confidence. When I had done, I could only say to him: 'On the Day of Judgement all will be familiar to you, for you have even guessed accurately at those sins which are known only to my confessors.'

But it is to Thee, Lord, that I offer my story—from first to last. I believe in Thee and Thy exquisite Compassion, of which Thou hast once more given me proof at the close of this Lent. Today, on this Good Friday, I beg of Thee who once said, 'Greater love hath no man than this, that a man lay down his life for his friends,' that Thou shouldest first of all forgive the faults and imperfections of my forty-nine years of life. Above all I have lacked faith in Thee. Born with an over-anxious temperament, I have often struggled alone to overcome my troubles without realizing Thy friendly presence! I reached a stage at which I did not think of Thee, or confide in Thee, until much later when the bitterness of the moment had passed. Not only was I in self-torment, but I was often afraid. Yes, afraid, in spite of the brave front I assumed. The brother monk who once said I was the 'acme of timid audacity' had the right idea.

I am insignificant, Lord, and very vulnerable. Many people have hurt me without realizing it, deceived by my apparent indifference, or by what they thought was my pride. I am no great personage. I am a child, so may I not be as a child? Grant me, Lord, as an Easter gift, the completely trusting soul of a child of God. Thy son, Peguy, wrote, 'Whosoever shall surrender himself, that man do I love, said God.' Without Thine aid, Lord, I am incapable of such faith. May my future life be an ever more complete surrender, drawing ever closer to Thee.

I have tried to devote myself, Lord, to those who hardly know Thee. I have tried to enter into brotherhood with them, with no aim beyond the achievement of that brotherhood. A young woman of twenty has lived near me for some six years and, as Thou knowest, she came to me this morning to ask that I should prepare her for baptism, something I had never broached to her. Lord, may it be ever thus. And may this saying always guide me : 'Be single of heart and good shall come to pass through you unawares.' I thank Thee for enabling me to make contact with those who have no faith. I thank Thee for allowing me to draw near them, to work with them, to open my heart to them and to see them opening theirs to me. It is rather the narrowness of believers that has always hurt me so much. For me, Lord, faith means a greater respect for the beliefs of others, and a greater love for all. It has been borne in on me a hundred times that one must impose nothing, try to gain nothing, but simply be. Grant me then to be Thy son, to know Thee better day by day, to grow ever nearer Thee, to pray better, to accept with better grace sacrifices both great and small : weariness, insomnia, pin-pricks, misunderstandings, jealousies, shortage of money, the thousand little setbacks of daily life. Enlighten those about me, unite the little company which has been entrusted to me, and whose disagreements distress me. Dear Lord, this prayer is wrung from the depth of a worn-out shell of a body. Weariness overwhelms everything else, makes the world look black, and every eager spirit dreads it.

At the close of this Lent I offer up my weariness to you, awaiting strength to free myself gradually from it. Make this man who has listened to the story of my life in some degree a prisoner-at-large of the truth, Thy truth. And see to it that his message and mine shall go forth as one to whisper to all our brethren—to all mankind—in all four corners of the world, that they should try to understand each other, love one another, help one another, because they are all the same, all equal, and all children of the same father.

P. DOMINIQUE PIRE, O.P.
Good Friday 1959

CHAPTER TWO

———————————————◆———————————————

Beginnings

WHEN *the youthful Rhine first breaks away from Lake Constance and turns towards Schaffhausen, it as yet carries only a light freight of swans and moorhens. Its banks, one German, the other Swiss, are close together.*

On the Swiss side slumber the score of houses that make up Gottlieben, the Hamlet of the Good God. It has an inn for solid citizens to stay in, the Hotel du Drachenburg, and opposite is the chateau which formerly sheltered, either at their own wish or under compulsion, a deposed Pope, John XXIII; a reformer destined for the stake, John Huss, and an adventurer en route to an imperial crown, Napoleon III. . . .

The inn is rich in old oak, leaded lights, and wrought iron. Above the windows which pass both the light and all the goings on outside through their bottle-glass filters, chimaera gargoyles spout out the rain like salamanders spitting fire. The roofs are shingled and the rooms are warm little cubby-holes, snug and secluded.

In one of them, panelled with red pine, the Reverend Father Pire, Nobel Prize-winner, is seated before a table of the fine wood of a fruit-tree, light smooth pearwood. With slight gestures he puts in order the pages of his life. Outside there is March sun and silence. If there were a Nobel prize for silence, Gottlieben would win it every time.

Tell my life-story? When I am still comparatively young? While I am still like an arrow shot into the air, unaware of the final mark it will reach? Where is it that this frail leaf is being blown by the breath of God?

It is Father Pire who speaks. He has come here to make a retreat, holding out his life to me like a skein of fine wool which we are to unravel together. He reeling off and I winding the ball, while the vibrant thread of memory links us.

Then, too, this is the first time I have looked back. It surprises me to realize, as I did just now, for how long I have been living a year or two ahead of time. This very evening I was drafting out my working plans for next year, even for the year after . . .

Besides, it takes a little effort to bring back my childhood. My pilgrim thoughts must turn back on themselves. In imagination I always see myself from behind as I plod along life's highway, but now I must, as it were, go on ahead, and lie in wait for my childhood self to come up out of the past . . .

My life . . .

Any man taking that for his title must inevitably begin his first chapter with the words: 'My mother . . .'

My mother's name is Berthe, Berthe Ravet. She was young when she bore me, for she had been married at eighteen. Georges Pire, my father, came from Namur, and was a schoolmaster at Leffe, in the Dinant suburbs. At twenty-two he met this pretty young girl with the coil of raven hair, then only sixteen or seventeen. He fell in love, married her on 26th December 1908 and a year later I was born.

My mother sometimes says to me: 'I used to play with you as if you were one of my dolls.' She was certainly young, and still is! She has kept her zest for life, her optimism, her positive outlook, and in this she is a complete contrast to my father with his quiet, methodical ways. He has always been mindful of those powerful deities, public opinion and social position, and the things that are, and are not, done. She has sailed along with all canvas spread, like a frigate in fine weather. The difference between them was apparent from the first day of their marriage, and is illustrated by an incident none of us children had known about until recently, when our parents celebrated their golden wedding. Mother had kept the secret fifty years, but on the anniversary she could no longer resist temptation, and out came the story at last! On the evening of their marriage, in spite of my father's punctuality, they had missed the honeymoon train. What a catastrophe in their bourgeois, provincial circle! My mother found it highly amusing, but my father was horrified. They would lose face completely if they showed themselves in the town on the morning after the marriage ceremony.

They stealthily took a room in the little hotel opposite Dinant station, got up while it was still pitch dark, and went off to take the first train from the next station, trudging through the snow with their suitcases ... That happened on 27th December 1908, and my mother waited fifty years to tell the story. Even half a century later my father could not see the funny side of it. Still less could my mother be brought to realize that it was her fault that they lost the train, and that such things really do matter ...

I was not an only child, there were seven of us, of whom four are still living. Nelly, who has five children of her own; Francoise, whom we nicknamed 'La Victoire', because she was born on the opening day of the great liberation offensive, 18th July 1918; and Charles, born in 1922. The first-born, I had come into the world on 10th February 1910 at

123 rue Saint-Pierre in Dinant. Since it had been a Thursday afternoon, always a half-holiday, my young schoolmaster father had been spared having to ask for a day off.

What did they christen me ? Georges—Charles—Clément —Ghislain. Names enough, or so I thought, but my father can prove by documentary evidence that I am also entitled to be called Eugène and Francois. Six christian names! Still, it's all one to me. I never use any of them. It is a long time now since I have been anything but Dominique, Father Dominique . . .

Like everyone else we have our family memories which come to the surface when we all gather on some sad or happy occasion.

There is the peaceful memory of my paternal grandmother, Eugénie-Leopoldine Brichard. At ninety-three, she is blind, and lives in retirement at Namur in the care of the Franciscan sisters. All the same, she insists on having the newspaper read to her and on having news of her grandson. She keeps watch on me . . .

Then there is the tragic memory of my maternal grandfather, François Ravet. He was a carpenter and had an instinct, a genius, for wood-carving. How many fine ceilings once emerged little by little from the piled wood-shavings of his workshop. All went up in flames with Dinant itself in August 1914, when on the 23rd of the month German troops set fire to 1,300 houses and shot 660 men of the town. My grandfather was killed before his own house. Two days before he had watched the boat which carried his daughter and son-in-law and his grandchildren away across the Meuse, and in the family recollections the old carpenter's last wave as he stood on the river bank is a treasured memory. Just his hand raised in a farewell salute, and the distant rumble of the cannon.

I was in that boat. Four-and-a-half years old, and still

weak from an attack of croup that June. My first memory is of myself in bed, heavy-headed. Nearby there is a small saucepan of hot water, and some silver tubes, for they have just performed a tracheotomy. It has been an emergency operation on the kitchen table, by the light of a single gas jet . . .

The scene becomes blurred. I am huddled in a cellar. The carrots I am eating make a crunching noise, and a shell whistles before embedding itself in the chandler's shop on the other side of the road. The horizon is red, and it is time we were away. Barbed wire cuts off the bridge over the Meuse, we are on the bank, we take the boat. My grandmother cannot bear to leave her home, my grandfather stays with her. There is fighting round about Dinant, and someone says: 'The French are re-taking the citadel by means of the little stairway.' I imagine the steep rock, the red-trousered troops, and the crooked bayonets among the greenery of the cliff. And the blood which will be streaming down those 408 steps. I am tired, my throat hurts. I walk, I sleep. We ride on a tram, we take a train, we spend two days and two nights in a goods wagon. We make a stop at Rennes, in Brittany, because 'little Georges is feverish'. People stare at us, are sorry for us, help us. I am a refugee, a D.P. But, I didn't know it then. I was neither to know it, nor fully understand it, until thirty-five years later when I saw my brothers of the camps . . .

My parents are now at Rennes in Brittany with their children, one convalescent and the other a babe in arms, but they have no money, and they have lost their suitcases, left behind Heaven knows where. The warm-hearted Bretons help them at once, give them somewhere to live and work to do. And what do I remember of all this? Pianos! Just pianos. The kindly people who sheltered us were manufacturers of them in a small way. Our particular benefactress,

Madame Bossard-Bonnel, sold them. Like Jean-Christophe wandering in the forest of sounds I was fascinated by them. I gazed at them in their solemn ranks, dressed for the most part in black, and each holding out four little copper arms bearing quivering candle sockets, but I went no further in my study of the piano. Worthy Madame Bossard-Bonnel was prudent as well as kindly and, no doubt in my honour, she locked all the lids.

Meanwhile, my father was looking for work. The suit-cases were gone, but he had managed to save his teaching diploma. A fair wind caught this paper sail and brought him before M. Dodu, the local school inspector, who had his headquarters at Rennes. On 9th September 1914 a Belgian teacher—my father—took the place of the French head-master at the village of Essé, who had been called up.

'Which do you prefer? Town or country?' they asked him. My father, because young Georges was still poorly, chose the country. I spent nearly four years at Essé and, curiously enough, the stay of this small Belgian did leave a trace or two. I have an old schoolfellow down there in Brit-tany, the Abbé René Pelhâte, now Rector at Ercé-sur-Ilet, who clearly remembers playing with me in the garden of Croix Rabot school. It seems that I was dressed in a blue-striped overall, which distinguished me from my comrades who wore black ones. And I used to fetch milk from the farm owned by little René's parents, carrying the can on my head, like Perrette, the milk-maid of La Fontaine's *Fables*.

I should soon be five, and I was put to school. My teacher was my father and my father was my teacher. I owe much to this blending of authority. Even today I manage my affairs with that same obsession for clear, exact accounts formerly instilled into me by my father's teaching.

Of course I was very strictly brought up. *Noblesse oblige*.

But apart from this general atmosphere, I remember from this time only holidays, trips out into the countryside, pancakes jumping in the frying-pan, and colts who jumped with equal liveliness in the fields. There were fishing expeditions, too, and I have never lost my love of angling. A photo taken in the summer of 1916 at Essé-sur-Seiche shows my mother in a white blouse and black skirt, and carrying a bag with double pockets. A big dog sits looking at the four fishermen in their straw hats and stiff, stand-up collars, and among them is my father, proudly holding a rod and line with a small fish dangling from it. The downcast child in the check pinafore, posing as if under punishment, is young Georges, in a temper because he was not allowed to hold the rod. My father had said no: I would not have kept still and the fish would have come out as a blur in the finished picture.

I am still delighted at the thought of going fishing. Not long ago, when the doctors recommended fresh air and exercise to defeat the constant insomnia which ten years of refugee work have inflicted on me, I chose to go canoeing and fishing on the Meuse. Friends offered me the right equipment, including a notable small stiffened cap in green felt, which is considered just the thing among Belgian fishermen at the moment. I do not think I shall ever wear it, for it would not look quite the thing among Dominicans, but when I look at it up there on my office shelf now and again it brings back the beauty of the river and the fresh breeze.

This photograph of 1916 certainly starts a train of memories, for it makes me think of all the fish I have caught over these last forty-five years, and I think of them with a degree of pleasure that is only slightly tinged with remorse. In particular there is a certain fishing expedition I undertook as a novice at the Dominican monastery of La Sarte. In the long vacation of 1930 Count and Countess d'A. put the hunting lodge of their Ardennes estate at the service of the monastery, and we were allowed to use it to give us a break in our long and tiring studies. On my walks in the park I had noticed a pretty, cascading stream where trout must abound, and when it was announced that the Prior was coming on a visit the next day—a Friday—all the elements of temptation were assembled, so I ventured to ask permission from the Countess to explore the stream. Permission was graciously granted, and soon afterwards the gamekeeper arrived with two rods ready prepared and a bucket: 'Here you are, Brother Dominique, everything you need. Are you sure the bucket is large enough?'

Having said this, with just the right touch of irony, the keeper went off on his rounds, and I made for the stream. On his return two hours later, no less than thirty-two trout were wriggling in Brother Dominique's bucket.

The Prior had fresh fish that Friday all right, but the Countess did not call on me to furnish her table on later fast days. No doubt she was not anxious to have to re-stock her stream . . .

But let's go back to Brittany. I was now six, and afflicted with all the cares that beset sensible little boys: homework, lessons, my catechism. My mother had very early begun my religious training, and communicated to me her piety, sincerity, and consciousness of a God who was peace-loving and gently kind, but also watchful. I still retain a vivid impression of the effect of my first confession, a feeling of having been cleansed. At about the same time, I also had my first intimation of human tragedy. Since we had left Dinant on the 21st August we had not heard of the massacre on the 23rd, but one of my uncles, visiting us on leave from the Belgian army, told my mother of her father's death. She wept, and it was her tears, rather than the account of the killing, that gave me some confused intuition of the suffering of mankind . . .

In 1917 the Belgian government at Le Havre sent my father to Normandy to supervise the schools of Laigle in the Department of the Orne. More than a thousand Belgian

refugees were in this area, the men working in the arma-
ment factories and their two hundred children studying in
four classes—one of them being young Georges, who might
have changed his school but was still in the charge of the
same master. However, I worked very well. After the Nobel
Prize award, my father made that very plain when giving
press interviews: 'He made steady progress, but naturally I
kept him very much under my eye.'

It was as if he would say: 'He may be forty-eight now,
but he still needs it.'

Did I? Perhaps. Let us see.

We lived in a little street close by the cathedral in which
the town crier's voice boomed majestically: 'Take heed . . .
The Mayor of Laigle, Pierre Chabot, wishes it known
that . . .'

That is all. Just the recollection of that all-powerful
voice, and my respect for the authoritative person in charge
of such a splendid drum.

I also remember the Spanish flu of 1917. I can still see the
hearses lining up before our house, waiting their turn for
absolution at the cathedral.

Another very different memory is of the birth of my
little sister Françoise, on the 18th June 1918: Françoise
'La Victoire'. I was then eight, and it was an age of dignity,
modesty, and decorum. One was not born, one 'arrived'.
Discretion was even carried to such a pitch that they
showed me in the courtyard the straw-lined box in which
Françoise had been delivered. It was no better than the
stories of storks and gooseberry bushes told today, for only
truth is good, needless to say.

One final memory of Brittany: that moving November
evening when we waited for the Armistice. We knew, we
children of the war, what that meant. They had told us all
about it: victory, the triumph of right over brute force . . .
And so we waited. Then all the bells began to ring, and their

reverberations have still not died away in my heart. On that evening, the bells added to their already supernatural power the ability to bring peace . . .

But I wander from my aim: the justification of my father's idea that he needed to keep me 'under his eye'.

Here we are at the close of 1918. We were leaving Normandy and going back to Belgium. Trunks were being packed, and dismal rumours circulated among the refugees.

After four years of occupation, Belgium was said to be stripped bare. Not only was clothing impossible to get, but thread, needles, and even buttons. Supplies must be obtained before leaving France. So father ordered a fine brown suit in 'pure wool'. Madness at sixty-five francs! Georges was very impressed by the preparations, as his mother sorted out their clothes. They would be taking only the newer ones. One evening his mother, after consideration, said to his father: 'Tomorrow, I'll take all the buttons off our old clothes. You never know. They might come in handy.' Young Georges overheard all this from his little room. All, that is, except the word 'old'. And he went off to sleep, lulled by a good resolution to be helpful to his mother.

By noon next day all the buttons were laid out on the kitchen table. Every one, even those from the brown suit. Today my father will insist I was a neat workman, cutting only the thread, and that I was a fine, brave little boy. For my part, I think I took off a piece of material with each button, and that despite my good intentions I came in for a beating. Anyway, I was amazed, convinced of having acted rightly . . .

We were soon back in our country, with Dinant in ruins, and with me enrolled in the 'khaki' class of the primary school at Leffe, in the suburbs. Here it was that my grandfather had been shot, and there were plaques everywhere recalling war-time atrocities. At the gasworks the Germans had thrown the bodies of the citizens of Dinant whom they had shot in among the white-hot coke . . . It was recorded on the wall.

Here there was a 'khaki' class, whereas in France classes had been named after the brighter colours . . . Dinant was a martyred town. Nothing had yet faded. Even the children breathed in the strange, implacable atmosphere. I have before me now my class photograph of 1919, all of us ranged in four rows with our arms crossed. There I am on the extreme right, with a celluloid collar and a huge knotted cravat with the ends floating loose. And, see! They have cut my fringe and so given me a thinker's forehead. My teacher, M. Wayens, is on the extreme right. He is still alive. A pupil, standing to attention in front of him, holds a little Belgian flag. In the front row two little ones hold up the well-known engraving of the 'Royal Dynasty', showing Queen Elizabeth, the royal children huddled up against her voluminous skirts; King Albert with a fine pre-1914 beard; Leopold II in a frock-coat and Leopold I in military uniform, both risen from the tomb with the express purpose of posing for the family picture. Four little button boots peep out beneath the frame. Finally, another pupil holds up a blackboard on which the master has chalked a message in beautiful English:

'Let us remember! If any district of Dinant has suffered more than the others from German barbarity, it is surely Leffe. Atrocious scenes were enacted here, to be followed by a mass slaughter. Out of a population of less than 1,400 inhabitants, Leffe mourns the death of 240 martyrs. How many orphans we have among us! Let us remember our heroes, fallen for their country!'

Such was the climate of thought in Dinant forty years ago. But I was nine years old. Dare I say that the sufferings of my country moved me less than the opening horizons of happiness, the overflowing joy, which the discovery of a tricycle on a rubbish dump near our house at Leffe gave me? Long ago as it was, I still relish that discovery. What grown man who was once a boy will not sympathize with me? That tricycle made the conquest of the universe seem a possibility. I was a king as I pedalled away.

I blush as I write this, for I think of little Anne Frank writing her journal at almost the same age. I dreamed only of my tricycle, but she took thought for the whole world. I was a child, and no more than a child. And I think that is what I am still . . .

Yet there are two other recollections of that time which sometimes come back to mind.

One is of a tree, a sturdy young willow, shooting up in what had once been the entrance-passage of the house where I was born, now a burnt-out ruin. I looked at it with awe. It seemed a wondrous mystery, and later I realized why. I had seen the triumph of life over death . . .

The other is of my mother, radiant with pleasure at having found in our looted home in that Leffe suburb a sprig of the orange blossom from her bridal wreath . . .

That is how my childhood comes back to me, just in detached flashes of recollection. Nothing is clearly defined, there is no steady development of theme. Just the memories of any ordinary little boy with no other interests and activities than the normal—religious duties, family life, school, and the innocent wonder of childhood. At nine I still believed in Father Christmas, and I set myself to please him so that he might send me a bicycle. You see, I still had my mind on wheels! As it turned out, Father Christmas almost refused, for the grave matter of the cinema had intervened.

For boys of my age in 1919 the cinema was an even greater wonder than the cycle. I longed to see a film. Did I say 'longed'? I was dying to see one, wasting away at the thought, and so much the more because my father had expressly forbidden me to. With the ideas of 1919 did he see damnation in it? I was never to know, and he has forgotten. The prohibition was all the more grievous because it was our own *curé*, himself and in person, who had given me the ticket which would admit me to a free performance at the hall where the film was reeled off by the turning of a handle. I fell to temptation. Late one afternoon I left the house, pushing a wheelbarrow loaded with wood which I was taking to some friends of ours. This was my excuse for going out! I then waited at a chum's home until the time the cinema opened—the hour of Charlot and Zigot, the stars of those days. Already uneasy, I became even more so when the lights in the room fused and plunged us into darkness. Not only was I oppressed by my own sense of guilt, but felt that even the elements were ranged against me in universal disapproval.

My chum's mother asked us to go and buy her some bread. It was dark when we went out, and to see our way along the alley we made a torch out of newspaper. I bumped into a passer-by, and in the light of my torch I recognized my father. He had been waiting for me . . . My unquestioning obedience, my sudden anxiety to stock up our friends with wood, must have raised some doubts in his mind. It was a dramatic moment, but I held my ground. Under cross-examination I only confirmed my dreadful purpose:

'Yes! I would have gone to the cinema.'

'And afterwards?'

'I don't know.'

'The knowledge that you were being disobedient and would be punished was not enough to stop you, wretched boy!'

'No! I would have gone to the cinema, and then thrown myself into the Meuse.'

Forty years ago, paternal authority and filial remorse did reach that pitch.

All the same, I got my cycle, even if Father Christmas did send a blue-pencilled reprimand with it.

That's the end of my childhood dreams. They were not so many, and all except one came true. For years I longed passionately for a Meccano set, and never got it. That is probably why I still stop in front of toyshop windows and gaze at the little shining metal bars and golden gear-wheels. I suppose I shall yield to temptation one day, just as I did with the cinema.

The reader over my shoulder now whispers:

Those childhood memories are all very well, Father. But don't you think that they lack something? How can I put it? Should not there be some glimpse of your inner life, the foundations of your Christian faith? Surely there must have been something of the kind even as early as this?

He says it in kindness, and of course he is right. Not to put too fine a point on it, all I have told up till now has not a very religious tinge. But what can I do about it? He did not know me as a child, and I think that as he looks at me he is too much influenced by my life as it is now. I am a priest, a Dominican father, who has tried to relieve a few of the many whose sufferings he has seen, and who has been given a Nobel Prize. What a difference all that makes to the way many people see me. They take the imaginary virtues they find in me as a mature man, and want to impose them on my infant self. Because I am now a priest, it follows that I must have been a juvenile saint! I still see myself from the same viewpoint as I always did and, I am sorry, but I have to disappoint them. My childhood was simple enough. I was merely a child, that is all, and I have not changed much. I had no problems, just the natural, easily accepted faith which any child has who is brought up by good, careful Catholic parents, and by teachers of the old school, in a somewhat limited way of life. Nothing more. No sudden insights, no visions, no tongues of fire! A child of God, I was swaddled in the linen of Holy Church, as most other children are. I was a Christian and a Catholic as naturally as I drew breath. Even my first communion was no different!

All I remember of this important occasion is that I had a velvet suit and a watch. I do not say that my belief was not fervent, but I kept my feet on the ground. It was the same with learning the catechism. Thousands of children have similar memories. There was the *curé* out in front, with the boys of the class ranged to one side and the girls to the other. We played tricks, made fun of the 'favourites', and when I sometimes meet in Dinant one of the little girls of my class, now a stately matron, our memories agree: we made the *curé*'s life a misery.

So then, there was nothing that was not very ordinary and even commonplace. I insist so much on this because my contacts with numerous reporters and would-be-biographers have been instructive. To listen to them, one would imagine that the world is ruled by a love of marvels; and they spend their lives in search of the stupendous. I disappointed them. There is nothing stupendous about me and my life has never been anything more than the rather slow current of a little stream which widens as it flows. All the same they tried to make me conform to their ideas, and confronted me with a choice: stained-glass sainthood or complete fall from grace. I do not think that is a choice I am ever likely to make.

Even so, I reached a turning point in my childhood when, at the age of eleven, I finished with the primary school at Leffe and entered the College of Bellevue at Dinant. It was an imposing establishment, the chief of the diocese, and nobly situated on the side of the steep hill facing the town. It was under clerical control, but with some lay teaching staff. The discipline was old-fashioned, to say the least, but it could hardly have been otherwise.

The Principal had been there nearly half a century and he thought, for example, that it was shocking for us to wear shorts and long grey woollen socks rolled over below the knee. He insisted on the uniform of the boys of his youth: black serge knickerbockers trimmed at the side with little silk-covered buttons and reaching the knee; and long black stockings coming well up into the knicker-bockers. At the end of his reign he had to surrender to English-style socks, but the iron entered his soul . . .

I can remember my first day at the college—not a pleas-ant thought. I had spoken in line, and had to stay behind. I felt deserted, alone, lost. I was afraid.

Fear. It was fear that dominated me throughout those long years. Fear of doing wrong, fear of being punished, fear of this and fear of that. I had a veritable complex of which the foundations had been laid at home under my father's severity. If only I had been able to see at the same time his underlying kindness, but I had not discernment enough for that! As I was saying, I was afraid. I had a little spirit lamp bobbing in front of my cycle, and one evening, on my way home from college, the wick was swamped and went out. A policeman pulled me up and reported me, and I was half-dead with fright. Even today I shudder at the thought; I can still point to the exact spot, within a foot or two, in the street where this disaster happened. My father succeeded in getting the offence overlooked, and what a man he seemed in my eyes from that moment! But I always stood in awe of him, paralysed by the image of him I had created. I hesitated to invite my friends home for fear of hearing him say, as he did one day when he was probably feeling out of sorts:

'What idiot is that ringing away at the door now !'

Happily, my mother's friendly cheeriness compensated the balance. She, in complete contrast, would have kept open house. She was delighted when the doorbell rang. It was something unexpected, and for her the unexpected always had charm. At moments like this my father would go off to do his accounts, and my mother welcome the excuse to defer doing hers till later.

Neither of them have changed since. Although they have celebrated their golden wedding, my father can still not understand why he married a woman who hates keeping household accounts.

But, returning to my college days, what sort of a student was I ? I am only too conscious that I was timid, a swot, and tried to curry favour. I was afraid of the big, hefty boys and the boisterous ones, trying to protect myself by being in their good books. I worked, not to excel, but because I was afraid of being scolded for bad work. The truth is, I was psychologically retarded, and the dogmatism of childhood still overlaid my critical faculty.

I owe my intellectual development to my studies in the classics and a sense of duty. I am infinitely grateful to my teachers, and particularly to Canon Nicholas, our splendid Superior. I did well and carried off prizes, having a mark of 93 per cent. when I reached the end of the course. But it was only in this field that I made this sort of progress, and worked intelligently. It was only my achievements here that made one of my professors say to my classmates : 'You will see: he is a methodical, conscientious worker. We shall hear more of him.'

The methodical and conscientious worker was seventeen, and faithfully adhered to the rules of middle-class behaviour for boys of his age : work hard, behave like a gentleman, and do not run the streets.

A fourth rule, peculiar to the college, was that we were not allowed to speak Walloon, even at home. At that period in Dinant, the patois was thought vulgar. I observed this rule too, and such was my general perfection that the master responsible for discipline invited me to his room, together with some other paragons. This was the pioneer age of radio, and we were privileged to wind inductance coils for him. I stopped dreaming about cycles, and set my heart on acquiring a fragment of crystal. This I never achieved, but I did gain third place in the final examinations. Of those in the first two places, one became a Jesuit, and the other a Master in Theology and Professor at the *Grand Séminaire de Namur*. The third is now a Dominican, and so I could go on down the list : *curé*, Capuchin friar, Carmelite monk, etc., since fourteen of the twenty-two boys of my year had a vocation.

So ended seventeen years of existence and twelve of schooling. I was still not so very far from the little boy who had carried that can of milk on his head back in Normandy. I trotted along the road of life full of fears and bursting with admiration.

The fears were for myself, the admiration for others.

The college chauffeur, who drove a huge F.N.[1] car with forged iron axles and a gleaming copper radiator, personified for me the might of all humanity when he majestically announced : 'I am going to let her flat out . . .' How powerful and how splendid he seemed !

I wanted to be like him, in command of the elements, but I have only succeeded in being at the beck and call of suffering.

[1] Fabrique Nationale d'Armes de Guerre.

CHAPTER THREE

The Lasso of God

DO YOU KNOW, *Father, you are describing yourself as if you had been just an amiable little animal?*

I looked at him—the fine forehead, large nose, eyes at once merry and sad, and the bitter-sweetness of his expression. We were walking along the bank of the Rhine, and only the sighing of the reeds broke the silence. In the distance, on the German shore, a flock of snow-white sheep were scattered over the grass, and on our side was a typical machine-cultivated Swiss market-garden. A red March sun impartially warmed both sheep and market-gardeners.

Father Pire made no reply. As he walked slowly along, he was apparently only concerned with avoiding muddy puddles and picking out the dry spots for his great shoes. He was not wearing the voluminous white habit of his order which makes every gesture seem a winging into flight, but a travelling suit of dark grey, with a clerical collar, and he seemed to have shrunk. The reeds were above his head.

What are you trying to say?

His tone was preoccupied. I had to goad his diffidence a little.

I am trying to tell you that I think you are being too modest. How can it be true that for you, a classical scholar, the conquest of the universe lay in obtaining a few radio

34

*crystals? Can you really tell me that you would have liked
to become a chauffeur?*

*Father Pire laughed, and this seemed more promising. He
gave his shoes, those boots of a soldier of the heavenly
army, the benefit of a fine patch of new grass, and I could
hear in my mind the voice of his mother telling me: 'As a
boy Georges was kind to everyone and everything, even his
shoes. He polished them like mad.'*

I suppose it is rather an outline sketch than a fully
finished portrait that I have given you. But, suppose you try
reconstructing your soul as it was at the age of fifteen.

*But still, Father, you did use the word vocation when you
were speaking of your fellow-students. Now, let us talk of
your own, especially as you have just admitted that these
stories of your childhood have not been in keeping with
such an idea so far.*

*Father Pire was smiling still. I was cornering him and
ashamed of it, but I pressed my advantage. This was the
ultimate reason why we had come to shut ourselves up in
Gottlieben's encircling silence. For days past I had been
taking down the story of his life as it came in little bursts of
confidence, and now he was as tired of talking about himself
as I was of forcing him to talk. Closing his eyes, he pressed
his eyelids with his finger-tips, his face hidden in a familiar
gesture indicative of both weariness and the turning inward
of his thoughts.*

I thought very early of becoming a priest, he said slowly.
Yes, very early in the medley of studies which made up
those six years of devotion to the humanities. I wanted to
be either a priest or a doctor, nothing else appealed to me.
My mother had given us all a religious upbringing, my
sisters, my brother, and I. As a good little boy, I had absorbed it, and I wanted to do good. It was a mere senti-

mental fancy with no driving force behind it—a vague idea of benevolence. As far as work went, I was absorbed in my scholastic achievements which had become rather too much an end in themselves. On the spiritual side, I had an undeviating faith. I never experienced a crisis in passing from simple piety to adult belief. I myself had no problems, but I have since lived amidst the problems of others, surrounded both by believers of other faiths and by those with no faith at all, and I have felt as much at home with both as a fish in water. This was because God in his kindness had subjected me to two enlightening experiences. I had received an education deeply nationalist in tone and strongly Catholic, but my nationalist principles were shed when I was sent to Rome to come into contact with Christians from all over the world. Later, in the scout movement, I had to organize rallies in co-operation with Protestant and Jewish chaplains, and my eyes were opened to a conception of international collaboration between the Christian Churches, through which my faith in God was strengthened and enlarged by the contrast of what I had now seen with what I had previously known. Intellectual contact with the Dominicans also played its part—that 'reasoned assent' which St. Peter described.

But I am anticipating. Towards the end of my classical studies I was mentally awakened by one of the college superintendents, a priest, who brought together a little group for theological discussion. We were studying the *Summa Theologica* of St. Thomas Aquinas, and this developed in me a taste for theology. At the same time, and unconsciously, I also developed a taste for the theological life, the Dominican way of life, in spite of the fact that I had then never seen a Dominican and knew nothing of the order, even of the purpose of their mission.

But, Father, when you had completed your studies at the

college, were not you enrolled at the Petit Séminaire de Floreffe, where the secular clergy are trained.

It is true, answered Father Pire, there is an apparent contradiction in that, but it can be explained by my youth, and by that unformulated will to good that inspired me, clear as to its goal but undecided on the road to reach it. Perhaps my father's caution influenced me, for he had undoubtedly been much perturbed when his son, so young and ignorant of life, had mentioned the word 'monastery'. I think he advised the seminary as more appropriate to our time than the novitiate in order to leave the future uncommitted, and so that we might wait to see if my youthful resolution would persist. After all, I was not yet seventeen. My letter telling my parents of my wish to become a religious is dated 6th December, the feast day of St. Nicholas, 1926. I was in the classical sixth . . .

But then my parents must have told you all this. Their memories are often more accurate than mine. For them it was a practical matter, while I was still living in youthful dreams . . .

Father Pire had sat down on a bench facing the Rhine. In the distance smoke rose from the village chimneys. I left him, going over in my mind the simple and moving story that Madame Pire had told me. I saw again that lovable woman with her fine head of grey hair and the laughing innocence of her beautiful eyes, and heard her clear, friendly voice. She was cooking dinner in the great kitchen of the house at Dinant, and as her nimble fingers prepared the salad she said:

'He was a good boy. Very religious, but in rather a solitary way. I was almost envious of his inner devotional life. He used to impose penances on himself. Oh, those childhood penances! Once at carnival time, and at Dinant the

carnival is really something, the procession was to pass beneath our own windows. Young Georges pledged himself to stay in his room, and he did, too.

'That letter of his from college cost me some tears. I would have liked him to be a doctor, but still, I wouldn't influence him. It seemed to me that a priestly vocation is too grave a thing to be interfered with lightly. I don't think that any of his teachers really put any pressure on him, it just happened. Yet, somehow, I couldn't see my son as a priest. I argued, for my heart wasn't in it.

' "Why do you want to be a priest?" I said.

' "God in His goodness has called me."

' "No one has influenced you?"

' "No one."

' "And so, you want to enter a seminary."

' "Never. I don't want to be a curé."

'What was it that he wanted then? When he went to the Abbey of Maredsous to make a retreat for five days, he was home again by the end of the second day.

' "Why have you come back?" I asked him. "I don't want to go to a place like that. They spend too much time praying."

'Then he thought for a while. He spent three or four days meditating in his room. And then:

' "I am going to make a retreat at La Trappe," he announced.

'Off he went, and was back even quicker this time, poor little chap. But then he went to stay at La Sarte. He took to the atmosphere there as a cat takes to a saucer of milk, my boy did.

'He came away delighted.

' "That's it!" he cried. "That's where I must go!"

'And he didn't change his mind either!'

'Yet, Madame Pire, he still enrolled at the Petit Séminaire, didn't he?'

She spared a glance for the joint she had roasting, before she said softly: 'That's my Georges for you! Who knows whether he didn't mistrust his own enthusiasm? Whether he didn't want to test his vocation and the strength of his will by an attempt at renunciation? Whether he wished not to make his entry into the spiritual life a matter of undiluted joy? That may have seemed to him too easy a way. Only he can ever tell us how it was.'

'And so you gave your full consent at last?'

'Yes, but not without a struggle: and that's leaving out of account the exasperating sympathy I was offered by all my friends and acquaintances. The things they said! That time, for example, when someone remarked: "He is far too handsome to be a curé." I jumped up and said: "I suppose you think the good God only wants the ugly ones to serve him."'

And Madame Pire set about laying the table.

And now I saw Father Pire, in my mind's eye, no longer sitting on a bench on the river bank, but back in his office. Over there is his mail, over here his breviary, and within easy reach the big notebook that he always has with him. In his tiny, almost illegible hand he sets down in it in detail, his projects, his plans, his thoughts. In this way he fixes on what is essential. Some time ago I was able to leaf through in his office at Huy the notebooks covering his first visit to the refugee camps. A close-lined record dating from 1949, violet ink ceaselessly criss-crossing the page.

All the misery of mankind was inscribed in it, in that slightly tremulous hand.

Running over the page, a phrase or two here and there caught the eye:

Hard Core . . . 80,000 tuberculosis cases . . . Every age, every kind of misery . . . the Cossack camp, in existence ten years . . . people without shoes. Some without even feet . . . an old man of ninety making fishing nets . . . you may burn down the huts. You can't burn the memory of them from people's hearts . . . Sloboda—a Russian 'village' with ten children, might as well say ten rabbits in such conditions . . . camp-life is vagrancy in a confined area . . . even the air isn't free. The ventilators in these bunker hotels . . . to think that my feebleness is the only weapon available against these living conditions, this filth, this selfishness . . .

And now Father Pire is writing: there are instructions to his staff at Huy to be given, outside contacts to be maintained, moral and religious guidance to be imparted. This untiring weaver is lengthening the piece of cloth which is his life even as I grope to find the thread with which it began.

The sun is setting and it grows cold. Round about us the reeds toss their heads.

'Father, tell me about La Sarte, this monastery which sent you back home in such raptures.'

At once, he draws himself up, youthful colour returning to his lips and cheeks. It is as if some invisible servant had lifted for a moment from his shoulders the burden of cares and sorrows that Father Pire continually carries.

My friend the priest at the College of Bellevue, the superintendent who presented his little theological ideas so attractively, suggested that I and some of my fellow students should go and make a three-day retreat at La Sarte. I had never before seen a Dominican, and I knew nothing of the organization and mission of this preaching order. We cycled the thirty-or-so miles from Dinant to Huy, following the river Meuse, and when I got to the monastery, built on high ground with a magnificent view over the valley, I could not have pedalled another inch.

The cramp which disables imprudent cycling champions had immobilized my legs: I had drunk a glass of beer when we stopped half-way. As always, the sacred and the profane went hand in hand.

So there I was at the door of the monastery and, as usual, scared—even terrified—at the necessity of meeting strangers. But, instead of monastic severity, I found the fathers wreathed in smiles. Sister Cécile, a contemporary of St. Dominic, said of him that his was a joyous, fragrant faith. And so I found it at La Sarte.

They showed us our rooms on the first floor and the retreat began, or rather three days of uproarious holiday. We did everything but make a retreat, and the fathers were just as bad as we were. I can still see all our fifteen cycles, their tyres deflated, hoisted up in the library, and the battles we used to have in the garden with the August windfalls as ammunition.

There were some wonderful characters there, especially the brother of one of the monks who could climb a ladder using only his hands. After getting up early to go to matins, we used to play cards. Once I stole the trousers of a boy who has since bought some new ones and become a famous surgeon. You can see from all this just how profound my call to be a Dominican was. But at seventeen one is carried away. The secret of our excitement was simple, we had been overwhelmed by the air of joyous thanksgiving at the monastery, by the gentleness and kindness we found there. We were as if struck by lightning, and three of us were 'killed' on the spot. One even went so far as to order his Jesuit's cassock straightaway, and later our college superintendent also joined us.

What was it that conquered me? Well, I had thought to find statues and I had found human beings. Dominicans have great clarity of vision as far as this world is concerned. They form no priestly caste apart from it. What enthralled me was not the influence of a man who could perform marvels up a ladder, but the irradiating intellectual magnanimity typical of the order. It was the lasso of God.

On my return home, my friend the priest was met by my mother with the words: 'Monsieur L'Abbé, you are going to steal my son away from me.' She sensed the shadow of the monastery—that word which holds such terrors for mothers, because it means separation. When a boy becomes a secular priest, he is not lost to his mother, for he can take holidays and she can pay him visits in his living. The monastery is quite a different matter. When I entered, it was two years, all but a month, before I saw my home again. During that period of nine years of study, novices have only six days' leave every two years, and these are merely 'allowed' and not taken as of right.

I have great respect for these ways we inherit from the Middle Ages, and which are not so irrelevant to our racketing modern age. The monasteries have preserved the art of contemplation.

But, Father, what answer did the Abbé give your mother?

He simply said: 'And if it is God's will, Madame?'

Myself, I knew that it was God's will, and I still remember my feeling of exaltation. I was like a climber who has found the route to the summit of a mountain.

Even so, when the September of 1927 came round, you went off to Floreffe just the same.

Yes. I was already committed to that. I wanted time for reflection, too, and it would have seemed too much like taking the easiest way if I had entered on the religious life by the pleasantest road. Anyway, I had promised my father this period of delay.

There I was then at the seminary, and pretty unhappy life was in that strict atmosphere. It was also the first time that I had been a boarder. At the seminary six years of the Humanities were followed by a year of philosophy. But, whereas my comrades from the College of Bellevue went on to the freedom of the university and the smoking of their first pipes, I went back to a rigid discipline which might have worked well with sixth formers, but was too narrow for young men. I had been up in the blue, and now I was back in a boarding school with a lot of other urchins. So, I counted the days, marking them by lines on tree trunks, and each line crossed through meaning the holidays were one day nearer. I did plenty of studying, too. Here it was that I made my first contact with the aridities of philosophy and logic. To me they seemed a sort of supertrigonometry, and I believe I learnt it all parrot-fashion, so you see what a fine philosopher I should have made. The moral atmosphere was not a favourable one either. Prejudice is everywhere, and when it was known that two of us seminarists wished to enter the Dominican Order, we were nicknamed 'the men in white' and generally put through it. There was a lecture, I recall, on 'the difference between the life of secular priests and that of other religious'.

An odd enough subject, for are we not all bound to live in truth and charity? Two things that were said, I remember, cut me to the heart : 'I prefer to be of the order of Our Lord, rather than to follow any saint, whomever he might be' and 'Dominicans? Mere shooting stars . . . They just talk big. Like their prototype, Lacordaire.'

But fortunately, the shooting stars of La Sarte wrote comfortingly, and I held firm.

We were still at the Drachenburg and supper was just over. At neighbouring tables hefty Swiss, enlivened by the local wines, were carrying on light conversation in stentorian voices. It was time to send Father Pire off to bed, and once in his room this eminent theologian, this winner of

the Nobel Peace Prize, would not disdain a detective
novel . . .

Of course, I am only joking when I talk of 'sending him
off'. He would have decided that for himself, as he hates
noise. I have seen him turn the hotel upside down, rouse the
other guests and the chambermaids, and change his room
to another floor, just because of noises in the water-pipe in
the wall. He unceasingly tries to find quiet in order that he
may be able to sleep.

Every night feverish insomnia sits by his pillow, and
every night the battalions of his thoughts begin their
march. He reviews his work, criticizes it, and yet once
more compares his own small strength—as he sees it—with
the immeasurable load of human suffering. The refugees
appear in sad procession and he counts them in dismay.
How can they all be helped?

Already it is dawn again, but that dispels nothing. Mass
is celebrated. A full day's work follows. Then night once
more. In the darkness conscience glows into life again, just
as a fire does when the cold air of morning strikes it. The
familiar anguish, as right as it is painful, accompanies him
like some dreaded friend, or rather, beats within him like
a second heart . . .

Now he was getting up from the table. During the meal
he had been youthfully gay, recapturing the mood without
any apparent effort, perhaps owing to the influence of the
monastic rule for periods of recreation.

Suddenly, a stray word had reminded him of his cares,
and he had withdrawn into himself, his light extinguished.
In his mind all the correspondence, all the costing figures
for a new European Village were simmering. There is nothing for it but to wait for a break in his concentration, or
else to go to his aid.

While he ordered his camomile tea, the latest of the
thousand cures for insomnia he had been recommended, I

sat thinking about him, his unassuming manner, his trust-
ing way of taking me, as it were arm-in-arm, along the road
of his life. We had just reached the crucial point, for to-
morrow he would say to me with his usual preciseness:

'On the 14th September, 1928, I entered the monastery.'

At that moment he was like a drop of water. It gradually
grows, takes shape, detaches itself, and falls. The sea re-
ceives it and absorbs it—the immense sea.

What was this preaching order in which young Georges
was about to lose himself in order to find himself?

The Dominicans originated in the thirteenth century, in
1216. At this period the life of the Church had deteriorated
in Western Europe: comfortable living had led to the loss of
its sense of responsibility and of true Christian direction.
Habitually accustomed to luxury, the clergy cared little to
proclaim the teaching of Christ in all the fulness of its
severity. The great intellectual drive once possessed by the
abbeys had almost exhausted itself: the Word was no longer
taught in its purity and morals were lax. In the part of
France in which Dominique was to lay the first foundations
of his order, there was a revival of various ancient heresies.
The Cathars, descendants of the Manichaeans, roamed
throughout Languedoc, and claimed for their creed all the
attributes of perfection, particularly poverty. The local
bishops and clergy were concerned only with the observ-
ance of external forms, having no aspirations to a deeper
appreciation of faith, or greater intellectual understanding.

It was then that the Dominican Order took shape. Its
members were to aid the bishops, receiving from them the
official charge to preach. Sent out among heretics who
claimed perfection, they included in their luggage a complete set of the neglected virtues, being particularly careful
to take with them poverty, which they and their twin

order, the Franciscans, were bound to observe throughout life.

So that they might be worthy preachers, they devoted most of their time to dryly austere, but life-giving study. Saint Dominic, their founder, with the inspiration of genius, despatched his first friars to all four corners of the intellectual and Christian world, dispersing his rising community to Rome, Bologna, Paris, Toulouse, and Cologne. In this way a revolution, parallel to that in the political world, took place in the Church in the thirteenth century.

Just as the feudal system was being replaced by a system of communes, the Dominicans were abandoning the seclusion of ancient and venerable abbeys to build their monasteries in the town centres. In an intellectual world busy reorganizing itself, this preaching order largely dropped the manual labour traditional for monks in order to devote themselves almost exclusively to the mental labour of study. But they retained from the past all that was applicable to the present: the life in common, mainspring of their religious life and work; the choral recitation of the Holy Office, an irreplacable means for the heralds of God to achieve a moment of contemplation; the internal organization of the monasteries, based on prayer, mortification, and poverty.

Thus the Dominicans showed their attachment to what was of lasting value in the traditional, while at the same time appearing as innovators. It was the aim of their order, not its spirit, which was different. They adopted the silence rule of an enclosed order, but in order to devote themselves to intellectual work. They emerged from it with the ardour of Crusaders to go out and teach the doctrine of Christ. This way of life was a radical innovation and, strange to say, the order has retained through the centuries the same elasticity of mind. The modern Dominican still possesses to an extraordinary degree an instinctive sense of how the

Church should adapt herself to the needs of the moment.

The preaching friars have as their motto Veritas—Truth.

For the Dominican, devotion to Christian Truth takes precedence over all else. As a preacher it is his mission to defend and teach the truth, the Christian Truth to the deeper understanding of which he has consecrated his life.

In the history of the order there are some names which stand out more than others.

Since its earliest days two men have defined its outlook and ideal. The first was St. Albert, called 'the Great' (1193–1280), a German whose encyclopaedic mind would bear comparison with the scientific brains of today. Physicist, mathematician, chemist, biologist, psychologist; anthropologist, man of science, and author of an amazing number of folio volumes, he acquired a prodigious amount of knowledge for that period. Yet, it all led him to become a theologian: he founded the chair in theology at the University of Cologne.

His pupil Thomas Aquinas (1225–74) was the most perfect example of this combined function of teaching and research entrusted to the Dominicans. A consummate master of theology, he presented the Church with a fully elaborated science of the subject, such as had been non-existent before his time. From a material and rather irreverent standpoint, one might say he produced a theological Encyclopaedia Britannica in thirty-four volumes.

The life of Catherine of Siena (1347–80), among other Dominican mystics, is proof that this passion for Truth leads not to aridity but to a closer approach to God. It would be difficult to find a greater example of the living paradox the Dominican is than this young girl, a contemplative Sister who died at thirty-three, to whom we owe the most beautiful mystic writings. They were written between two journeys at Avignon and at Rome, whither she was able to persuade the exiled Pope, Gregory XI, to return.

Another famous member of the order is Francisco de Vittoria (1483–1546), to whom we owe the first treatise on human rights. In the era of the rise of colonialism, it was naturally to a Dominican that it fell to bring theology to bear on this new problem. A comparison, such as never yet seems to have been made, would perhaps reveal that the Atlantic Charter of 1948, introduced nothing which had not already been proclaimed in this old treatise on international law. The same humanitarian conception guided Bartolomé de las Casas (1474–1566), who was intent on putting into practice the doctrine of the brotherhood of man, and vigorously came to the defence of the American Indians, those D.P.'s of the sixteenth century.

And then there is the long sequence of the 'singers' of God, the great preachers, from Saint Dominic himself to Père Carré today, not forgetting impetuous Vincent Ferrier (fl. 1419) and Lacordaire (1802–61) in between. Fra Angelico, too, who painted Truth in his frescoes, was also a Dominican.

The order has had its darker periods, when it was responsible for terrible things, was sometimes hard and cruel, according to the temper of the times, when only the completely submissive man was allowed to find grace.

But the centuries pass and this preaching order, seven hundred years old, still has a role to play and plays it. From its foundation it has retained the white habit and black cloak which were once the dress of the poor. Today this costume serves to recall the purity and joyous austerity which go hand in hand with Christian Truth and, undoubtedly, with every other kind of Truth . . .

CHAPTER FOUR

---◆---

The Wide Tonsure

THERE IS NO POINT *in looking too long at La Sarte from the outside. It is not exactly beautiful. That is understandable, for in Belgium architects are seldom chosen for their talent.*

Personal friendship, or the colour of a man's politics, are the things that count. The worthy fellow who built La Sarte some decades since had neither taste nor sympathy with the monastic way of life. The fact that he was related to the Prior had to compensate for everything . . . All he succeeded in producing was an arid-looking boarding school, with an endless series of dormer windows. Yet the presence of the monks has mellowed it. The great corridors are beautified by silence, and the too steep roofs lend themselves to the sound of pealing bells . . .

Books in thousands form a tapestry for the walls of the cells. Chance glimpses through open doors reveal figures in broad white habits bent over a work-table, bowed over a prie-dieu, or just enjoying a pipe in the midst of a blue fog.

There is the distant sound of the Holy Office, or the voices of Fathers at work with their classes. The door-keeper, a little, rosy-cheeked old man with silver hair and sky-blue eyes, scurries with a distracted air from the entrance hall to the parlour, from the parlour to the Prior and from the Prior all over the place.

He supervises the comings-in and goings-out. Visits are made in the parlour, furnished with ancient mahogany, the gift of a parishioner. How touching the doyleys and the oval table look!

The 'goings-out' are many, as befits a preaching order. Sometimes it is a youth in khaki uniform, swinging a small brown suitcase: a novice fit for military service, returning to barracks after leave.

For those who have entered the monastery when very young, this is the grand test, and not all of them are proof against this abrupt lunge back into ordinary life. That is to be expected. The fathers are prepared for it and wisely arrange that each survivor from the army medical service, in which the young monks serve as orderlies, shall spend an additional year, or even two, as a novice. Only those with a true vocation survive.

Often the monastery will seem deserted, and one has to go down to the refectory at mealtimes in order to surprise the white bees in their hive. This is a lengthy, rectangular room paved in blue and white tiles and with whitewashed walls. A crucifix hangs above the Prior's table at one end and, facing it at the other, is the serving hatch and lift connecting with the 'blessed' kitchen. For the rest, pitch-pine cupboards, poor and bare-looking furniture, clumsy porringers, and dull aluminium forks and spoons. The monks are ranged facing one another with their backs to the two long walls, and the Prior's table links the two 'wings' at the top end, just as artists depict the scene at the Last Supper.

Towards the other end of the room are the reader's chair and desk. Standing, the monks pray aloud, intone a psalm, bow long and low, with heads bent and hands resting on their knees. They uncurl slowly like some spotless wave.

Lost among his brother monks there today was Father Pire. Eyes closed, he prayed; bowed at the appropriate time; and obeyed the sound of the little bell like the rest. All the world had watched as he received the Nobel Peace Prize, or talked with the kings of Norway and Belgium. He had stirred the whole of Europe by his appeal for charity and brotherhood. He was pursued by press photographers and the great tried to lure him to receptions because a celebrity attracts all fashionable society. Mankind, which too often sees things in a too simplified fashion and sums up a man's worth in anecdotes, wanted to make him a star turn. At this moment, the star was seating himself at table, taking a glass from the wicker basket and filling it from the earthen-ware water jug. Pull your cowl over your forehead, Father Pire, as your brethren do, and kindly tuck your napkin round your neck to protect your white habit! Here come the spinach and hard-boiled eggs, carried in by the novices so quaintly dressed in their great kitchen aprons. Here are the cod, potatoes, and white sauce. And they won't be changing your porringer between courses!

Listen to the reader's voice, that special, sing-song in-tonation on one note, the recto tono: 'Life of Lincoln, Chapter Seventeen.' It rather recalls the convent school of your youth and infants learning their letters. But, eat up that heavy, sugared pancake in silence, Father Pire!

The Prior's little bell now rang the signal for grace, and once more one sees that breaking of a spotless wave as the brothers disperse.

Now you are about to pay your customary visit to your superior to render account and ask permission for all that you are about to do, for have you not made a vow of obedi-ence? Your life may belong to the poor, but your will be-longs to God and your superiors. Go back to your small cell, Father Dominique, draw the long yellow curtains over your bookshelves and sleep like the rest of the brethren. Should some noise awaken you tonight and make you sleepless, it does not matter whether you smile or grow impatient. Ex-perience will long ago have taught you that it is your *neighbour, Father X, cleaning out his room, even if it is three o'clock in the morning.*

Next day we met again in the monastery garden, the delightful garden one would expect a curé to have. Lawns blooming with jonquils, tulips, and forget-me-nots divided by walks into the shape of a cross. Shady shrubberies with winding paths, and a glory of cherry trees in the kitchen garden. A merry breeze from the Meuse set the habits of the novices flapping as they paced along chattering to each other, for the rule of silence is broken during recreation. The sun shone down and, over the monastery walls, the distance views were glorious. In the shade of a mass of lilac, the Fathers sat on rustic benches having coffee—not the fancy brew of a social gathering, but a clear, hot liquid served in bowls, with another bowl for the sugar.

Earth and sky; the monastery anchored on its plateau far from men, floating in space like a ship at sea amidst the breezes; the statue of the Virgin hovering on the roof's topmost pinnacle and stretching out her arms over the hills with their clouds of pink apple blossom; and from all this peace and simplicity came a sense of glowing, spiritual happiness which was overwhelming.

In the shelter of an arbour, Father Pire took up again the story of his youth.

I alighted, then, at Huy station on 14th September 1928, my only luggage a Bible and umbrella. In the square I saw another young man similarly equipped, and the fact that we both wore the prescribed uniform drew us together. He, too, was entering La Sarte. To reach the monastery we had to cross to the other side of the town and climb the hill, but we did not do it on foot in the way shown in old pictures where young men arrive dusty and weary to knock at the monastery door. Dear me, no. We took a taxi and I gave a

lavish tip, for I had no further use for money, I was liqui-
dating all my earlier life. My one big regret was a straw-
coloured trench coat of which I had been very fond, and
had had to leave at home.

Home . . . I had left it early in the afternoon. There had
been good-byes. I had hugged and kissed my mother and
father. She had wept . . . Then I had gone off alone to the
station.

As the monastery door opened I was met by the smile of
Father Dautrebande, just as in the days of those battles with
windfalls. We were taken to our rooms. How empty and
bare it all looked, the wash basin on its iron stand, the narrow wooden bed and the straw mattress! But it was my
room, and one can hollow out a place for oneself even in a
straw mattress.

Among the Dominicans life is highly individualized, each
having his own place from his novitiate until death. Something that greatly astonished me was the bareness of the
walls, all in whitewashed roughcast. Later, I also learnt to
apply roughcast, and to whitewash as well—miles of it. I
had come from a friendly house, hung throughout with
views of Dinant by my father, who was a past-master in
collecting things. The whole house was crammed with
knick-knacks, so familiar that they seemed to speak. Here,
it was like a desert.

By now it was dusk, and the coming night brought an
anguish of loneliness. In the evening the door of the novitiate quarters was always locked, according to rule, and I
could not conquer my panic. Did I want to escape? No, but
I did want to see if it was possible. I crept silently down-
stairs, and found a little window on the ground floor
through which I could squeeze if I tried. I went back to my
room, reassured.

My early memories of my novitiate are rather dim. It
was just another year of my youth. We found a great deal

to laugh about, and the thoughtless laughter of novices is not merely a literary fiction. Sometimes we had good cause. A Father might turn up at night office half asleep and wearing only his hood and scapular, having forgotten to put on his gown. This office in the middle of the night was a serious hardship, for we could not get off to sleep again after rising at twelve and coming back to bed an hour later. Nowadays it is said in the evening.

My first winter at La Sarte was terrible. Down in the valley the Meuse froze so hard you could cross it on foot, and the temperature in our quarters was twenty-six degrees below zero. Water no longer existed, and we had to break up ice and melt it in a bucket on the common-room stove. I made my first acquaintance with manual labour through the two hours a day which was the mild Dominican rule, and picked fruit, swept up leaves, cleaned the corridors, and laid and cleared the table. They provided me with the order's medieval habit, changed every fortnight and identical for all, whether novices, brothers, or Fathers. For the first month the novices tripped over the hems of their white habits, but they kept a watch on themselves and, after a time, automatically lifted it with their foot at each step— the 'monk's tread'. I had been tonsured, too. At this period the wide tonsure was the rule, leaving only a crown of hair three finger-breadths wide. The Father Novice-Masters gave instructions that our crowns should be extra narrow, in order to detach us the more completely from the world and its vanities. It was annoying, one could not even make a parting any more. The wide tonsure was given up during the Second World War, for monks scattered by the invasion and found wearing ordinary clothes were arrested as spies, as happened to me. After the war, our Superior considered that a state of emergency persisted. Moreover, the wearing of clerical dress or an ordinary suit, rendered necessary by much travelling and enquiries into social conditions, did not accord well with a medieval haircut, and so the wide tonsure was never re-adopted.

Also, I learned to fast. Not that the rule was severe. We had meat three times a week, cheese, eggs, fish, and vegetables.

At last, after a ten-day retreat and the taking of the habit, they gave me a new name, and I became Brother Henri Dominique—from the name of Dominic, my patron saint, and from that of my 'model', Henri Lacordaire. This monastic name remains a purely religious change, does not appear on one's identity papers, and the bank returns a cheque, even today, if I use the signature 'Father Dominique Pire'. Georges has to come to the rescue.

And so my life as a novice began. This meant new fields of study : the history of the order, the rubrics—that is the technique of the breviary and the Office—and Canon Law as it affected novices, especially as regards our vows of poverty, chastity, and obedience. It meant also a new rhythm of living. Our time was neatly divided into slices. This makes the novice more amenable. The time allowed for morning and evening recreation is short. Altogether, more stress is laid on the acquirement of religious knowledge than on becoming more closely acquainted with God.

Just the same, the novitiate remains the beginning of a spiritual life. We learnt to read—in the true sense of the word—and to meditate; neither very skilfully as yet. Though novices, we were still sixth-formers mentally, immature, and schoolboyish. We still liked a good gossip, and all the day's news finds its way to the novices' quarters in a monastery, just as surely as it does to the kitchen in a barracks.

Communal life under a strict rule makes one over-sensitive. One becomes a trifle introspective, and rather self-centred; one asks oneself silly questions about brotherly love: 'Brother So-and-so scowled at me today. Why was that, I wonder?'

On the other hand how earnestly we prayed, and what overwhelming joy and serenity it brought! We lived up to the saying: 'Novices look holy and aren't. Students are neither holy nor look it. The young Fathers are, but don't look it. The old Fathers are both holy and look it.' I can still see the way I used to hold my head, slightly inclined, at 'five to twelve' as it were, and my clear-eyed gaze . . .

When we were careless, we were punished, more typically by the *Venia* in which the novice making apology and asking for pardon stretches out on the ground and does not rise until the Superior knocks on his stall. Occasions for the *Venia* were frequent, for every novice, whether in the choir or the refectory, plays a public part. If you start off a psalm badly when it comes to your turn, half the choir follow you, and if you do not begin the antiphon on cue the singing comes to a halt. One should be penitent about such things! In the refectory there are faults in serving at table and in reading. Reading aloud and the use of the *recto tono* are important exercises for future preachers. Ah, that *recto tono*! It is neither easy to acquire nor sustain this single-toned delivery which is intended to lead its hearers to sacrifice and renunciation, but must at the same time successfully compete with the clatter of plates and dishes made by sixty people at table. Oddly enough, the Dominicans of Italy do not practise it.

The 'corrector' at the table used to prick his ears and break in with: 'You mustn't say Broglie; pronounce it Breuil . . .'

Accidents in serving at table, of course, might happen to anyone: a pile of plates slipping, a soup-tureen upset . . .

Once, when the bishop was on a visit, I distinguished myself in this way. He dined with us in the refectory, wearing a magnificent violet sash. Offering him the dish with my left hand, I held the sauce-boat in my right, at the same time admiring the beautiful sash. Alas, I should have done better to watch what I was doing with my right hand! The sauce was pouring respectfully over My Lord Bishop's shoulder, down his chest, and all over that moiré ribbon. He was soaked, but was kind enough to say not a word, though his forbearance availed me nothing : one of the Master Fathers had seen everything. What a lecture I got! In the meantime the beautiful sash went off for cleaning to a devoted lady in the neighbourhood.

On the first Wednesday of every month, we had a big, group outing. Off we went with knapsacks on our backs, covering six to ten miles, and eating our picnic lunch with some country *curé* before turning home. What appetites we had! And then, every two or three months, one's family would arrive in the monastery parlour and spend the day. Hampers of home-made cakes would appear, and surprise packets of home news . . .

All was eagerly devoured, except for the hampers.

What else do I particularly remember of my novitiate ? Well, there was the matter of one's correspondence. Letters written at the monastery are subject to the Superior's inspection, throughout one's life as a monk, except for those written by Masters in Theology, who are supposed to be wise men. The same favour is extended to my correspondence about my work, but only because there is so much of it. In principle, the Superior is entitled to open all incoming and outgoing mail. One day, when I was already a priest, I ran into trouble. A venerable Superior, as far advanced in years as he was behind the times, called me in and scolded me : ,What are you doing, writing to a young girl and calling her "My dearest Dear (*Ma chère Biche*)" ?' The good Father had confused the words 'dear' and 'deer', not noticing that the letter was addressed to a Guide-captain, and he had not a clue as to how we used animal names.

In my first year I had made a place for myself. Just as my body had created a comfortable hollow in my straw mattress, so my soul had found its spiritual nest. I looked forward to a lifetime devoted to good, but always in a dreamy sentimental way. It was a vision of 'the fragrant faith' of Sister Cécile . . .

I took my first vows on 23rd September 1929. These were for three years. At the end of the third year, everyone is free to choose, and this choice is as much a matter for the Prior as for the novice. It is as important that there should be an opportunity for the latter to renounce the monastic life without fuss, as that the former should be able to advise that it be renounced. For if you are not really in your element there, the balance of life in the whole monastery can be destroyed.

The ceremony at which the vows are taken is very brief. With my hands resting on a missal laid on the knees of the Father Prior, I pledged myself to poverty, chastity, and obedience. The first vow is often merely a confirmation of existing circumstances, it is the third which offers the real difficulty.

So, I took the plunge into three more years of study. I had to re-learn half the philosophy I had swallowed up at a gulp at Floreffe, including that pet abomination of mine, logic. Still, I was two years older now, and this time it was my mind as well as my memory which was at work. What really discouraged me always was abstract thought, the dry-as-dust abstract.

That is why I liked theology so much. God is concrete. The speculative left me cold, and I was attracted above all by action. I am no intellectual : I have a little intelligence perhaps, but no intellectualism. My brothers of the order are much more sharp-witted than I ! Let us say that mine is the natural philosophy of 'common sense'. Mind you, my aversion to abstract formulas is not because I am afraid of them, but because I am afraid of bypassing reality . . .

Twelve terms then passed in hard work. Sometimes there were a few days holiday, and it was in one of these that the incident of the noble count's thirty-two trout has its place. It was a time of tranquil toil.

My life, too, was like a trout-stream. I was studying, and I had a good opinion of myself. I was a thought critical in my approach, but only in a playful fashion. My consciousness of reality was always there in the background.

Then, on 23rd September 1932, the time came to make my solemn profession. The same vows, but now they were final. I hesitated not a moment, and though no credit is due to me on that ground, it is not always so. Some people only pass this point with difficulty, by reason of their character. I remember one novice who gave up, and went off shouting: 'One has no more freedom here than a worm.' Others make their retreat in good order, and become admirable fathers of families. Then, too, between the lock gates of the simple and the final vows, stretches the period of military service and the problem of resurgent liberty.

I bound myself not merely with confidence, but with enthusiasm. I had been spared the transition to the army in an odd fashion. As I was a plodder I had my recipes for endurance, chief of which was to devour not only my lessons but the meals, so I had to stimulate my appetite. A young Dominican is not very knowledgeable in the matter of aperitifs. I had adopted mustard! I crammed myself with food to such an extent at exam. time, after which the interview with the recruiting board was to follow immediately, that the result of my little manœuvre was that I had a serious outbreak of skin trouble. The officers of the board, after one disgusted look, exempted me on grounds of 'skin disease'. A week later I was happy and well again, but my record card followed after me like a curse and stopped my being called up in 1940. I was for ever officially contagious!

At the end of the second year of my philosophical studies, I went home to my parents' for six days' holiday, the first time in twenty-three months. It was wonderful, but disconcerting. For example, it was strange to find myself in the familiar surroundings of my childhood dressed in my voluminous white habit; to walk down the staircase instead of sliding down the bannisters! And when I went out, the strained attitude of the neighbours, the respect for something which they did not quite understand! Some were even proud of me. I myself was only conscious of a vague disquiet, which compelled me to self-examination. And so, 'an averagely good subject', I continued my slow development. For me, it was not yet the full growth of spring, I could not be really said to exist.

CHAPTER FIVE

---◆---

'I Became a Priest as
Naturally as an Apple Ripens . . .'

WE HAD BEEN DRIVING for hours along the winding
roads of Bavaria, that country of green mountains, which
are like a Tyrolean hat for shape and colour. The day was
dying—a moment Father Pire chooses for meditation—and
I was driving his medium-sized American car, chosen for its
combination of comfort and unostentatious line. This pilgrim of Europe, who had already covered about 124,000
miles in his journeys from camp to camp, and village to
village, needs comfort. His journeys, made for the most part
alone, are tiring—often a hundred leagues in a day, with a
conference or working party every evening.

As for lack of ostentation, Father Pire has brought it to a
fine art. He has had all the chrome painted black, because
the idea of entering refugee camps at the wheel of a gleaming automobile shocked him, seeming an insult to misery.

'I might as well have a big cigar and a check suit as well,'
he said. Since then, the people of Europe have watched this
strange car go by, more gloomy than a hearse, but driven by
the apostle of the life of light.

I drove and Father Pire meditated. Sometimes, on an ex-
clamation from him, I braked and drew to a halt—I was

well trained. He had seen a herd of deer grazing on the out-skirts of a wood, and the sight had touched him. He, too, would have made a friend of Gubbio's wolf. This Dominican has a Franciscan soul.

We had just come from Bregenz, in Austria, where Father Pire had been visiting one of his villages. All the villagers had crowded round him. As usual, they thrust their babies into his arms, confided their joys to his heart, and loaded his mind with their money worries. He carried away with him the impression of a living hamlet which had taken root and was about to flower. He was delighted, as heartened as the villagers themselves.

He was wearing his travelling suit again now, and the beautiful white habit was back in his suitcase, decorated with the imprints of little hands sticky with sweets.

We had a long journey before us, since he had to be in Munich that evening and as I took the umpteenth turn of the road, I began thinking about our biographical alliance. Now that this winner of the Nobel Peace Prize was caught up again among the practical problems of aiding Displaced Persons, how was I to take his thoughts back once more over twenty-five years. The other day we had got as far as the end of his novitiate at the monastery of La Sarte, but the thread had been broken. Tomorrow he would be off travel-ling again, abandoning me with calm good humour, but he had meanwhile prepared for me the next stage in this chase after bygone days, in which he was at the same time the hunter and the hunted.

In this way I met the people who had known him as a child in Dinant, on a visit to his parents' home with its pleasant smell of coffee, oranges, and beeswax. And what a home it was, and what people they all were!

Father Pire's birthplace is set in the cliffs of Dinant. They had to cut away the rock-face to make room for it, and its roof is at one in its steep slope with the cliffside as it runs up towards the citadel. From the windows of the kitchen and drawing-room the eye leaps like a salmon up a cascade of flower-covered grass, a great creamy fall, with the sonorously named Tour Taravisée—a medieval ruin—rising from it.

From her beautiful, countrified-looking rôtisserie—electricity has been installed, but they have left undisturbed the gas-burner and its little chains—Madame Pire, the 'very youthful mother', can at the same time keep an eye both on her savoury stews and her songbirds: canaries, bullfinches, siskins, finches, and golden pheasants. She gives the tomtits of the hillside free lodgings, hollowed-out logs or nesting boxes shaped like a clock, the symbolic 'Heart Open to the World', and even a sputnik! Beyond the yard is a little garden where swings once went to and fro, but now the children have left the nest, and only the birds remain.

Madame Pire talks of her son with verve. She has the gift of making things live, this mother of the Nobel Prize Winner. Listening to her, one sees the image of Father Pire melt, fade away with bewildering speed, lost in maternal feeling, and when one finds him again at the other end of the telescope, he is only 'Little Georges'. And here he is, as his mother sees him:

'I was only nineteen when he was born. The midwife had forbidden me to eat on the great day, but I had such a good pea soup on the hob! I gave myself a whole bowl full, and I didn't do wrong either. Little Georges has always loved soup ever since.

'His birth cost me fifteen francs, according to the tariff, and I don't regret the money. His weight? Eight pounds. Make a note of that: it will interest the English and Americans, for they love statistics. After the award of the Nobel Prize, all the English-speaking reporters who flocked to Huy began by taking his measurements.

'He arrived at five-thirty in the afternoon. My first-born!

And the happiness he brought was as new as the pains had been. He was very easy to rear, I never had another like him, and such a beautiful child! People used to stop me as I pushed his pram and tell me so, and I didn't find it hard to believe them.

'His grandfather wept for joy when he saw him, his tears falling on the cradle. "We could do with half a dozen like that," he said.

'The only thing he ever broke was a gilt-crystal decanter we were fond of. But, since it was my fault for leaving it where his little hands could reach, it was me who came in for a scolding from his father.

'He was obstinate, and would stand in the corner an hour and a half for some little fault, rather than say he was sorry.

'He used to tease his sisters, and would say, "I don't like girls." In the evening he wouldn't go to sleep unless he had given them a little slap, and, when he was sent to bed first as a precautionary measure, he used to lie in wait for them on the landing.

'He was a little jealous when the first of his sisters was born, and told us to "Put her up in the attic."

'At home, he used to keep the cellar tidy and cut wood. In the street, he would refuse to hold my hand, saying, "I'm too big for that."

'How did we punish him? We used to put him in the corner, as I said just now, and then, when he was bigger, we gave him lines. He would write out twenty times to a page: "I must tell the truth." Though it wasn't really that he lied, he just didn't want to confess his naughtiness and kept silent.

'One of his daily tricks was putting the radio out of order. While we were out, he would take it to pieces and reassemble it; but he always had some bits left over and used to throw them into the stove.

'What was the greatest treat we could give him? Letting

Above. The Pire family: Father, Mother and the children. Little Georges is at his father's right. *Left*. Georges Pire in 1928, before he entered the monastery. *Below*. Brother Dominique as a student in Rome

Above. At the time of celebrating his first Mass, at Dinant, 22nd July 1937 —the Reverend Father Dominique among the angels. *Right.* 1944: Chaplain in the "Secret Army" of the Resistance.

The D. P. camps: ancient barracks and human distress (*"Aid to Displaced Persons" Photos*)

Aerial view of the European Village at Bregenz, Austria *(Photo by Spang, Bregenz)*

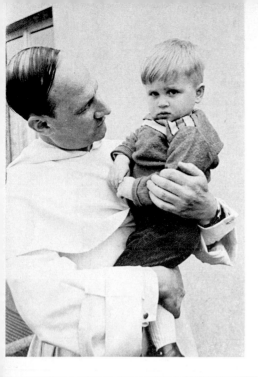

Left. Father Pire holding two-year-old Ceslaw Averon, first child born in the first European Village, at Aix-la-Chappelle. "Thanks to me," Father Pire said, "he was born free." *("Aid to Displaced Persons" Photo). Below.* the European Village at Aix-la-Chappelle. *(Photo by Sepp Linckens, Bad-Aachen)*

Above. The Nansen European Village at Berchem-Sainte-Agathe, near Brussels *(Photo by Xhardez, Brussels). Right.* Father Pire laying the first stone of the Anne Frank European Village, 31st May 1959. Behind him, with head bowed, is the father of Anne Frank. *(Photo from* General-Anzeiger der Stadt Wuppertal)

"He will be able to dream in peace. . . ." *(Photo by Belga, Brussels)*

Father Pire at the window of his little office at Huy. At upper left, the "hanging garden." *(Photo from* La Meuse, *Liege)*

Father Pire at work in his office on the Rue du Marché, at Huy.
(Photo by B. Moosbrugger, Zurich)

Left. In the garden of the Monastery of La Sarte with the Prior, the Reverend Father Delville *(Photo by B. Moosbrugger, Zurich). Below.* King Baudouin of Belgium receives Father Pire at his palace in Brussels *(Photo © Belga, Brussels)*

Above. Gunnar Jahn, President of the Nobel Committee, confers the Nobel Peace Prize on Father Pire, 10th December 1958. *(Photo from* Arbeiderbladet, *Oslo). Below.* The gold medal of the Nobel Peace Prize. *(Photo by J. Schaeger, Huy)*

"What is God's will in planting in me this disquiet? . . ." *(Photo by B. Moosbrugger, Zurich)*

him cook his own supper. Even now, he has a knack with spaghetti.

'Once when Father Christmas brought the children a toy grocer's shop, they quarrelled over it, because everyone wanted to be the customers and no one wanted to be the counter assistant.

'Did he use to write to us? Frequently, and punctiliously. Young as he was, he already had a mania for accuracy. He not merely dated his letters, but followed his signature "Georges" with a note: "It is two minutes past eight."

'And, innocent as he was, he was cunning, too. In 1923 when he was thirteen and was at home in Dinant while we were on holiday, he wrote:

My dear parents,

I should be very pleased if you would bring me back a pen-knife. Not a girl's, but a good, strong one, and really sharp. In drawing-class my teacher gave me a lecture because I had not got a pen-knife, and went on to say that I couldn't be a real man without one . . .

'He had his pen-knife.

'He was a good trencherman, and thought nothing of seven slices of bread and butter in the morning.

'He was obliging and willingly did the shopping. Even today when he comes to Dinant he will go and choose the Sunday cakes at the pastrycook's, and come back across the town with the carton dangling on its string from his fingers. If the Nobel Foundation knew that . . .

'He was a practical joker, too, and has tied me to my chair a hundred times . . .

'He used to collect stamps and cigar bands . . .

'With you I can refer to him quite easily as "he" or just "Georges", but when visitors came after the Nobel Prize award I found myself getting quite pompous. Every moment I was calling my own son: "The Father."

'And I am not altogether sorry when he is tired or ill, for then he is mine again . . .'

Someone rang the bell. It was Sister Auguste, of the Sisters of Christian Doctrine, who came in. Eighty-three years old, come summer, she had a web of wrinkles under her white hood, and had been Superior of the school at Dinant for fifty-seven years. Not only had Georges been her pupil, but also his mother. Everything came easily to the good sister, the teaching of weaving, embroidering on card-board, and the art of plaiting little strips of pink and green stuff into ornamental offerings to some small saint.

'I had him in my class in 1914 when he was four. I taught elocution and singing to sixty children. Georges was affec-tionate and tried hard. He sang well . . .'

'Tell me, Sister, what did he sing?'

'Well, do you know "Cloud, oh lovely cloud . . ."?' And Sister Auguste, in a tiny voice, frail but true, sang:

> Nuage, beau nuage
> Qui passes triomphant,
> Sans cesse tu voyages
> Disait un jeune enfant . . .
>
> Ne pourrais-tu descendre
> Et t'approcher d'ici?
> Ne pourrais-tu m'apprendre
> A voyager aussi?
>
> (Cloud, oh lovely cloud
> Going proudly on your way,
> Ceaselessly you journey—
> A little child did say.
>
> Couldn't you come down
> And float towards us here?
> Couldn't you teach me, too,
> To journey far and near?)

'*He won his first good mark for that.*'

Sister Auguste was in grand form. Anecdotes followed one after another like the beads on a rosary: 'He used to choose only well-behaved friends; he was cured of croup by a fragment from a relic of St. Thérèse of Lisieux which I made him take in a little milk; one day he drew the Bayard Rock on his slate. He took great pains, but it still looked like a potato. And then he had his favourite round-dance, "The Dove-cote", which we used to sing at recreation time.' *Sister Auguste held out her hands, as if to make a ring, and sang:*

> Le pigeonnier est bien ouvert
> Pigeons, pigeons, que l'on s'envole!
> Ils s'envolent vers les prés verts,
> La troupe entière batifole!

> (The dove-cote now is open wide
> Pigeons, pigeons, let's fly away!
> The whole flock fly to meadows green,
> Tumbling and romping on their way.)

It is a lovely old rhyme and her heart was in it. Sister Auguste was radiant. Never in her life had she told a lie, and she would swear that the beautiful green crown of the Nobel Prizewinner was there in the place of honour underneath a glass cover in the classroom of Little Georges forty-five years ago. He had earned it already . . .

'And what did you say, Sister, when he was awarded the prize at Oslo?'

Under the hood her wrinkles gathered into a beautiful smile.

'I heard it on the radio. I wasn't surprised, but I was so pleased I could have danced.'

'But, you didn't?'

Sister Auguste, eighty-three this summer, gathered her black cape round her, and murmured with a start.

'But . . . I don't know how to dance . . .'

Nineteen more miles on the meter, with three stops to watch the deer. My thoughts came back to the road we were travelling, to Bavaria, and to Father Pire sitting at my side. Having seen him a moment ago in the class of Sister Auguste, I was almost surprised to find him a grown man, but those child-like eyes were reassuring. All the same, we had covered the studies and simple pleasures of his novitiate, what else was there? I had it! Brother Henri Dominique had been a practical joker at the monastery, but he had not said anything to me about it. It had been one of the venerable Fathers who had let me into the secret of his tricks a day or so ago. I sighed, and assumed an air of discontent.

'What's the matter, Hugues, my friend?'

I said nothing, but by now Father Pire was worried and insisted:

'Something is the matter, tell me!'

'I had not . . .' *I gave a gesture of weariness.* 'I had not thought that you would conceal things from me.'
Indignation almost stifled him.

'I conceal things? What have I concealed from you?'

'There's no need to go on, Father, I know the truth.'

'But, what do you know?'

'You drive me to it then? So be it . . .'
'Who was it who used to slip spoons into the pockets of

*the aged fathers at the monastery, and then call out, "Stop
thief!"?*

*'Who used to stuff the cowls of his brother monks with
bits of paper, so that when they drew them over their heads
at meal-times a shower of confetti fell in their soup?'*

*Father Pire laughed and admitted the indictment. This
scrupulous man had already been beginning an examination
of his conscience. In imagination, we were back at La Sarte.
The black car was once more a parlour, a place to talk. And
while the stars kindled their fires on high, Father Pire's
former life once more came welling up, leaving far behind
us the innocent jokes of the monastery.*

The half-way mark, he said, I was twenty-two, still in my
novitiate, but with four years study of philosophy behind
me, counting the year at Floreffe.

Now I was to leave for Rome.

Why? Holy Church had published a new *Ratio Studi-
orum*—regulations for theological studies. Henceforth, to
attain the rank of doctor in theology, one must take certain
additional courses of study which, at the time of this reform,
were only available in a few large institutions. By tradition,
we Dominicans always went for our advanced studies
either to the University of Fribourg in Switzerland or to the
Dominican University at Rome, called the Angelicum, after
St. Thomas, the 'Angelic Doctor'.

I was selected for Rome and set off with a brother monk,
a cantor who had come up from the Angelicum to spend a
holiday at La Sarte. I had never travelled, except in my
imagination. I was at a loss, overcome by my first contact
with the human antheap. As the train rolled on, I was very
conscious of the increasing miles between Belgium and
Italy. In Florence, at the Hotel du Lys Rouge, I was in such
a black state of depression that my companion said:

'Come on! Have a little something to cheer you up.'

There was a glass of red wine on the table, but I was afraid even of wine. 'Open the door,' I told him. Then, swallowing the whole glass at one gulp, as if it were a dose of medicine, I ran and threw myself on my bed, convinced that I was drunk.

Rome . . . I was not merely lost, I was distracted. The Student-Brotherhood, the *Studentat*, included men of seventeen different nationalities. Poles, Czechs, Yugoslavs, Spaniards. A whirl of languages and faces. I was absolutely bewildered, until now my only souvenir of my travels had been a photograph in which I see myself at the seaside, sitting on a sandcastle. The Prior was Dutch; the Father Tutor, French; the Rector of the University, Irish, and the teachers came from all over the world. The only things that were familiar were service at table and the reading aloud, but there were unexpected difficulties even here. With a hundred and fifty people to feed in a vast refectory, we had to yell at each other in Italian. Everything was new and unusual, even breakfast, which consisted of a big bowl of coffee and milk and some dry bread. No butter. And just think what 'No butter' means to a Belgian. At midday we had *pasta*, lentils and oil, and wine to drink. I had a very strict Pole sitting next to me, and when the Prior excused us because of the heat from eating, according to the rule, with our cowls over our heads, he complained: 'They don't keep the rule here!' Then, having tossed off his flask of wine, he begged for his neighbour's at the same time as he was making away with mine.

Once Christians used to be thrown to the lions in Rome. What happened to me was worse, because it was so ridiculous: with me it was mosquitoes. Every mosquito entering the Angelicum subscribed for a bite at Brother Pire; they bit me all over. I fought back, I exhausted every means of defence: muslin stretched over the ends of my iron bedstead, walnut leaves, incense, naphthalene, and every insecticide

there is. All to no purpose: I had sweet blood and the mosquitoes of Rome loved it. In the end I slept with every chink
in my windows stopped up, in heat like a Turkish bath. It
was no laughing matter, however, for they gave me Roman
Fever, which is simply malaria. I lost a stone in weight and
had to sit at my ordination, while the Father Superior kept
guard over me with an open bottle of menthol.

Our studies were conducted wholly in Latin. There is the
clear Latin of the French, and the voluble Latin of the
Italians, and when some of the latter were talking at top
speed you could not understand a word. And as for the
Latin of the Americans! How strange that sounded to European ears!

I felt very lonely, and this made me seek out my fellow-
Belgians, of whom there were a few in Rome, some seminarists, some priests, lay brothers, Benedictines, and Assump-
tionist Fathers. We used to gather for Mass in the Church of
St. Julien des Belges, or at the Embassy. It was Rome that
made me more fully aware of what my family and my
country meant to me: absence strengthened their hold.
Going so far away and being brought into contact with the
outside world, gave me a thorough shaking-up, broke
through my protective shell of dreams, and in this wider,
more varied setting, I consciously began to live.

My comrades helped me to emerge from my cocoon. I
remember a young Dominican who had been a Garde Noble
and a Marquis, the last of his line. A former scout chaplain,
he enticed all the Angelicum into the Alban Hills. How
wonderful the space, the silence, and the boundless horizon
seemed! I came down from among them strengthened, but
not yet a 'scout', and I did not become one till much later
when I was thirty-three.

In spite of these widened horizons, there was much else
to astonish me, such as the degree of freedom allowed on

this side of the Alps, at once more restricted and placing more confidence in us. For, although a priest might neither go out in the evening nor frequent cafés, he was allowed to go out for a walk, the *passegiata*, every day. I took advantage of the chance to explore Ancient Rome, and the museums, where lighthearted Roman piety gazed much more at ease than I, with my easily shocked northern sensibilities.

Theology opened her enlightening arms to me, and I saw God more clearly. I preferred ethics to dogma in this divine branch of knowledge, because I am a practical person, more attracted by principles applicable in practice than by abstract ideas. One of the intellectual shocks I received was a realization, through the study of comparative religion, how universal was the pursuit of Truth, and how great were those who had sometimes come near to touching it.

As a student, my results were average. I have already explained why: I am no intellectual! At the Angelicum, the hearth where the cream of all the religious orders of the Catholic world come to warm themselves; where the 'supernovae' of the scholastic constellations sparkled, I remained one of the crowd. No more, but certainly not less, for the mass was already the result of selection. I must be forgiven for displaying the pardonable pride of a good pupil!

My Christian education was quietly becoming more profound, but I was not yet scarred and haunted by the conception of humanity's misery. This thing which crept one day into my heart, and has wandered there for twenty years like a lost dog!

At Rome, I dreamed only of the apostolate. Something very much alive, but so naïve and neatly rounded in its limits! Just a gathering in of the good poor, good savages, and good agnostics. Squalor, moral filth, rancour, sluggishness, resignation in the face of injustice, all those evils

which weigh heavier than mountains—I never even sus-
pected their existence.

I was preparing for the priesthood. Through that I should
really become adult, I thought. I longed to save souls, to
communicate joy and warmth. Besides, being a priest brings
you closer to God, makes you a sharer in the Redemption.
I had all the enormous fervour of the youthful priest, un-
tarnished as yet by habit, that insidious spiritual slumber . . .

I was very new to it all, very eager . . .

I had also to study the rites of the Mass, working alone in
a small room as in a laboratory. And, how anxious I was on
those first occasions to make no mistakes. Thus, I became a
priest, without any crisis and with the wisdom of a child—
just as an apple ripens.

I was ordained first sub-deacon, and then deacon, in 1933,
at St. John Lateran. My ordination as priest took place on
14th July 1934 at the Basilica of St. Ignatius, at the hands
of a Capuchin bishop. It was moving to be ordained in
Rome, lost in a crowd of young priests from every country
—the grain of God, gathered up ready for sowing afar.

We shared in the Universality of Rome. I said my first
Mass the following day at the church of St. Sabine.

On the 17th July I left Italy, reached the monastery on
the 18th, and on the 23rd July said my first parochial Mass
at Leffe, the Dinant suburb. It was the parish of my parents,
who were celebrating their silver wedding that very day.

A moment of radiant happiness: the sum of all possible
happiness.

According to custom, the clergy and my brothers at the
monastery came to fetch me from my home. In front was a
procession of schoolchildren led by nuns, and the little girls
in white, with big angels' wings fastened to their backs, held
themselves very straight as is proper on such an occasion.
Banners, and garlands of leaves and flowers, swung to and
fro across the street and in front of the church. Behind the

clergy walked a crowd of friends, the good people of the neighbourhood. Then came my father, very grave in his morning-coat, and my mother, clutching the arm of a sturdy parishioner with her right hand, and a handkerchief with her left—a handkerchief for her tears of joy.

I hardly saw anything of all this until I looked at the photographs later. I was up in the clouds, my hands clasped to prevent my prayer flying away too soon. It was like a glimpse of paradise.

I came back to earth in the afternoon when I listened to a relative, Abbé X, being forgiving about my having entered a monastery. Yes, actually pardoning me for having done so. I had forgotten that he had said to me six years before, and very rudely in the stress of the moment : 'So, you prefer to tuck your thumbs in your sleeves in the depths of a cloister ! You haven't the courage for the back-breaking work of the secular clergy.'

I only recall this in all humility, and as a warning. The conviction that one is doing more and better work than other people is a destructive factor among men, even within the Church. Neither regular nor secular clergy are always blameless in the way they talk of such things. And yet, we are fellow-labourers all. What matter whether we use the tractor, the spade, or the hoe ?

CHAPTER SIX

---◆---

Changes and Transformations

A N D N O W , *another of our conversations at Huy, in the
administrative offices of the Aid for Displaced Persons in
the rue du Marché; an H.Q. spread over several adjoining
houses. Doors have been cut through walls, bridges thrown
across gaps, but nothing brings the floors on a level with
one another. It is a labyrinth more complex than that of
Daedalus, because of the staircases. They go running
straight up, or twisting round, everywhere, and even Father
Pire's office is a sort of landing, hanging between earth and
sky. There is a steep climb up to it, and seraphim go up and
down these steps, just as they did on Jacob's ladder—those
devoted souls, Father Pire's staff.*

*A certain spiral staircase, followed by two further
crooked steps difficult to see in the dim light, makes a
famous trap. You cannot count yourself one of the household until you have missed your footing here and tumbled
down a flight.*

*On the ground floor is the store of clothing and medi-
cines. A white bird was flitting among the forest of coat-
hangers. Father Pire had just been inspecting the gifts. Alas,
the consignments of linen, clothes and shoes are sometimes
disappointing, since, for some people, generosity and charity
are the same as getting rid of what they do not want. They
give to the poor as they would throw out things for the*

*dustman. Now and again something in good condition, but
if it happens to be a top-hat, how can one send that out to
the camps? Spring, the time when attics are cleared out, is
particularly productive of such false munificence.*

*There was none of this trouble in the case of the medi-
cines. The amount of them was something to wonder at, but
all are needed, for a Home for Old People swallows up an
extraordinary quantity of laxatives and cough mixtures.
One can do nothing but put a good face on it, and send out
the reinforcements of tar pills. These black battalions
always meet with a good reception.*

Father Pire dragged me skywards to his office.

Now, where was I in my story?

*You had just returned from Rome, Father, after your
ordination as priest.*
*He closed his eyes, and I could imagine his thoughts re-
turning along the stream of his life with the arrow-swift
flight of a kingfisher.*

I was now a priest, he said. But I had quickly to remind
myself that I was still a student, and what a crisis a doc-
torate in theology can present! For two years I laboured
on my thesis, for I must confess that I am not very well
equipped for writing a book of any sort, nor even finding
a subject. I first of all thought of a thesis on the difference
between Mercy and Justice, taking as my starting-point
the saying of St. Thomas Aquinas: 'Mercy is in some sort
the completion of Justice.' I wasted three months pondering
over that. Then my professor provided me with the basis
for a moral thesis on 'Apatheia' ($A\pi\alpha\theta\epsilon\iota\alpha$), that is to say the
condition of a man devoid of all passions, and with entire
mastery through his reason over all his emotions. For the
Stoics Apatheia was the *nec plus ultra*, the supreme goal of

all moral endeavour. I did some research into the opinion of second-century theologians on this idea, and especially St. Clement of Alexandria, himself a philosopher who had become a Christian convert. I discovered that he had taken over into his theology everything that he considered worth while in the Stoic creed, which had involved him in some very curious feats of reasoning. For example: 'Since Christ is perfect, he must exemplify in himself everything that makes a perfect man, and as Apatheia is the height of perfection, one must eliminate from the life of Christ all emotional feeling. Consequently, when He wept before the tomb of Lazarus, this was only a pretence, in order to put Himself on the same level as mankind.'

I did not find it difficult to prove that Apatheia is not only unattainable, but far from representing a desirable ideal is a purely destructive conception. Still, though it may not have been difficult, it certainly took me a very long time!

At last, in July 1936, the maintenance of my thesis took place. First of all I was questioned in theology for two and a half hours by five professors, each taking their turn for half an hour. Then we came to my Apatheia, still before the same five professors. This is when the student has his own back, and the specialist knowledge of the writer of the monograph outwits the generalized omniscience of the examiners!

At length, after having vowed before the High Altar to be faithful to Thomist theology, I was declared 'wedded to truth' and capped with the three-cornered biretta.

I was twenty-six, and well pleased in return to my monastery at La Sarte with my studies completed and, in particular, to be rid of moral philosophy. Good news awaited me: I would be instructing the Dominican Brothers there in moral philosophy.

And that is what I did, glad in spite of everything to escape having to lecture on logic which I liked even less. But I was a little sad just the same. I had a lingering regret that I could not lead a life of active dedication. I felt drawn rather to Apostolic work than teaching. But I pulled myself together : obedience should be given in the spirit not only in the letter. I accepted my professorship, and to prove to myself my wholeheartedness in doing so, I decided to specialize and went away for a year to the Catholic University at Louvain.

And that completed a full ten years of study after your having left school, Father?

That is right, ten years! At Louvain I began by undergoing my examination as a confessor, based on the practical ethics I had studied at the Angelicum. There I was again before five professors : first the problem under consideration was re-stated, then the case was examined, and finally came the judgement. It is a difficult, scrupulously conducted examination, but it confers on the priest a power of which one cannot think without being deeply moved. The confessor is a judge, but an accountable judge . . . I remember the first confessions I received. On the one hand, confession is a confiding in God, on the other, a means of exercising spiritual influence, sometimes to a tremendous degree, on a human being. One can do so much good. It is the supreme opportunity for individual action, and for me that is more important than anything else, I have not much faith in mass efforts.

I preached my first sermon at La Toussaint in 1936, in a Wallonian village. My voice struggled against the silence— a spiritual as well as bodily silence—and I trembled with anxiety to break through and in distress at failing.

There is a Dominican monastery at Louvain, and I lived there under a peaceful inundation of work. I had to absorb in two years a four-year course of lectures, but it was very pleasant, just the same, for I was not required to take the final examination. I could work in my own way, though always under the obligation to neglect nothing.

It was at this period that I felt the prick of the spur for the first time, and underwent my first spiritual transformation. In a green valley near the town nestled a chateau where the *Soeurs Missionaires de l'Enfance* looked after destitute children. I often went there, and I shall never forget the way those little children used to look round whenever I entered any of the rooms. It was a long, slow look that mingled uneasiness, resignation, hope, and an air of waiting for something. What was it they waited for, these little ones? Why did they turn their heads like that every time a door opened? They were being cared for in a kind, motherly way, so why this sudden welling up of an unspoken misery?

A sudden resolution seized me; I must do something about it. I must myself plumb the depths of the poverty, as so many others had done, and not only understand it, but wipe it out if I could. I looked into every possible remedy, but not until thirteen years later did I find the real cure, simply an abundance of love for humanity.

And from that time onward his work bore fruit . . .

In July 1937 he returned to his monastery to teach, and many novices had him for professor, some of whom have since become his superiors. He seems to have been a hard examiner, but when they told him so, many years later, it astonished him· had he not taught ethics, 'that is to say, the basis of life itself', who could be ignorant of such a course of study as that?

As priest, professor, and sociologist, he came in touch with youth. Perhaps subconsciously remembering the time when he was himself sixteen, and Faith, Hope, and Charity had held meetings in the superintendent's small office at the College of Bellevue, he started a little theological circle. He also concerned himself with feminine theologians, the Girl-

Guides of Huy and Brussels, teaching, or rather explaining theology to them in exchange for lessons in scouting. His period of initiation was lengthy, and the doctor in theology took more than five years to become worthy, not this time of a three-cornered biretta, but of that emblem of the proficient Scout—a pen-knife with twenty blades.

At last, in 1943, they gave him a 'jungle' name. He was to be called 'Tenacious White-Fang', which, although the scout leaders did not realize it, was symbolic. Had not St. Dominic's mother in a dream seen her son in the shape of a dog racing round the world with a lighted torch held between his teeth?

But let us listen to Father Pire's account of his life as a scout-leader in training.

It was at Christmas 1940 that I set about it in earnest. I had read all about Baden-Powell, but had not accepted everything without reservation. Indeed, *Homo Scouticus*, mistaking the extraneous detail for the essential, and going through life with his pipe tucked in the top of his ribbed socks, was no ideal for me! I remembered too vividly an old barrister scout-master I had known, with clusters of badges all over him, and great hairy legs beneath his little khaki shorts.

No, I valued Scouting for its friendly, cordial contacts and especially for the packs of Wolf-cubs, and the camps, big and small. I had made my Scout promise, but it was intolerable to have no 'diploma', so they bundled me into a camp-school in 1943. At thirty-three I had to compete with lads of seventeen or eighteen in climbing, following trails, learning morse, crossing brooks on stepping-stones, and tying knots. I could not make head or tail of those knots, and never learnt anything except how to untie them. On the other hand, I shone when it came to cooking, and in neatness and cleanliness. My palliasse, and my corner with its decoration of foliage, earned me commendation. The Scouts forgot that I had had practice in making straw mattresses from the age of fifteen.

In short, in spite of the camp being one in which such slow progress was generally made that it was known as 'Camp Tenderfoot', I became 'Tenacious White-Fang' and received the 'Gilwell' badge for my rank as a qualified leader. I had filled the gaps in my scouting knowledge, and could hold up my head again! To my Wolf-cubs I was no longer like a Minister in civilian dress reviewing soldiers in uniform.

During the summer of 1938 Father Pire established at Huy a small playground, at which the monitors were his Girl-Guide theologians. All on a budget of 800 francs.[1] And from this developed a second project. After the holidays were over, the girls kept in touch with the children when they returned to school. They saw the poverty of some of the homes, lent a hand, and so created the beginnings of a Family Mutual Aid service.

Father Pire put a great deal of work into it, in addition to the demands made on him by his work as a lecturer. Suddenly, from a simple request for advice made by one of his Guide-captains, arose reflections which prompted a second transformation in him.

These young girls, he said, truly Christian, but engaged in this 'neutral' Scout Movement, were anxious to maintain their spiritual life. On the other hand, their contact with a movement embracing all faiths, had given them a respect for the consciences of others. The problem could be summed up: 'You are a Scout-mistress and a Catholic. You yourself live with God, yet cannot make your faith accepted by others,' how should a Catholic behave in pluralist

---

[1] The Belgian franc is worth approximately twopence.

surroundings? I came to the conclusion that the believer does his duty if he strives unceasingly to perfect his inner life. His silent example will exert an enlightening influence, but in order to achieve its maximum power, it must be free from any desire to proselytize. This is because Christian perfection should be sought as an end in itself, and secondly because an aggressive apostolate cannot achieve deep and lasting result. How mistaken are those who claim that: 'Pears must be "forced" to make them ripen.'

Ideally speaking, the believer and still more the priest, should desire that each individual soul may attain to a full perception of the Truth. I do believe that a higher, independent, objective Truth exists, but there is also another and subjective Truth, which is our personal perception of objective Truth. St. Thomas asked himself 'whether one may follow a conscience which is, *in good faith*, in error, a conscience which is absolutely unaware that it is in error', and he decided that 'if anyone believes, in good faith, that it is wrong to serve Christ, and then serves him, he sins'.

All of us live within our own truth. All of us must also live with a certain spiritual loyalty that must urge us to make our subjective Truth objective, by constant questioning in the depths of our heart. We must also compare our subjective Truth with that perceived by others: this comparison can only lead us to a great respect for their good faith.

Above all, never doubt but that this confidence of yours will very often touch the person with whom you are having the discussion, as much as if you presented him with a gift. He will be encouraged to deepen his own search after Truth. And an honest doubter is worth more than a lukewarm believer!

In short, Father, I said to him one day, you believe there is a degree of unity among all men.

Yes, but it is a unity concealed in men's innermost consciences. A unity beneath the eye of God.

Then, there is, in the world, a kind of boundless, unor-
ganized community?

Yes. That of all true men and women. Long ago, they
were known as the invisible Church.

And could this community be organized?

No one can say whether this may be on the plane of faith:
perhaps an answer will be given from on high. But on
another plane, that of the human community, there is a
universal wish (or at least the seeds of such a wish have
germinated everywhere), a warm universal wish to find a
practical basis for a common life together. Jacques Mari-
tain has called it 'a temporal or secular faith', not a religious
faith, but a combination of the good principles honoured
by all civilized men. Everyone who thinks that life is worth
the trouble of living, that there is such a thing as human
diginity, and that Humanity goes forward to a goal, can be
moved by a spirit brotherhood, compassion, and human
generosity.
The Christian will see in that the law of God; the non-
Christian will find in it the joy of obeying the law of his
own conscience. Briefly, even accepting the hypothesis
which would make religious creeds permanently divided
into their own watertight compartments. a hypothesis I do
not accept, men would still share a common destiny, a
sense of reverence, and a respect for the liberty of others—
and of what incomparable value these are !

But what can be the focus of all this goodwill?

Those who are in pain and distress. If suffering is a

privilege, it gives rise to another as rich and sweeter-scented: compassion. To aid the suffering is both to ennoble them and ourselves, and the crux of the matter is to bring about some action, to transform goodwill into something concrete, to convert intention into deed. How much longer are we to hesitate before this Rubicon? For twenty years I have known what lies on the other side: pain to be soothed away, frozen hearts to be melted, loving-kindness to one's neighbour to be practised. This once established and the work set in train, who could then make it a reproach to me that I foster in my Catholic priest's soul the conviction that all men of goodwill are bound invisibly to the Church? What matter if, at the same time, I stand among the ranks of the universal and invincible army of those who revolt against Evil.

Such was the next transformation undergone by Father Pire: he had become acquainted with Divine Justice. He had glimpsed not only human injustice, but at the same time something bringing mankind towards a linking of arms in unity.

While he dreamed of a 'linking arms', however, war broke out.

In the early stage, from September 1939 until May 1940 Belgians referred, not to being on a war footing, but to being on 'a footing of intensified peace'—Pied de Paix Renforcé —*four hundred thousand men were sent on a fantastic, enforced holiday to play cards on the frontiers, and on the 10th of May the game was lost for the whole world.*

When the Germans arrived at La Sarte they found only the abandoned monastery. Even the Bursar had been mobilized since the preceding autumn as Chaplain of a regiment of the Chasseurs Ardennais. And Father Pire, formerly invalided out and still on the discharged list by the comic reason of his famous 'Contagious' record-card, tramped the length of the machine-gunned roads along with a million other helpless Belgians. Like every other citizen between eighteen and thirty-five, he had received orders to make his way to France.

Like the rest he was hungry, frightened, and tottering with fatigue. Rumours would run like wildfire through the crowds of French and Belgians, prompting sudden panic, and one of these was quite inextinguishable—the belief that German spies and parachutists had disguised themselves as ecclesiastics. This was why the monks of La Sarte had been advised to wear civilian dress but, unfortunately, they still retained the tonsure and were consequently as suspect to the Germans as they were to the Allies.

Father Pire, who at first accompanied the Huy Red Cross as it withdrew towards France, was sheltered on his arrival at Grammont by the nuns. Even in that peaceful community, however, there was a gnawing fear of espionage, and his tonsure, dusty civilian suit, and his silence in his weariness all had their effect. He was denounced to the authorities! The police came swaggering along to the convent to arrest this German spy, and he was in genuine danger of death. Others less fortunate did pay with their lives in those days for the momentary stupidity of mankind.

Happily, Father Pire burst out in amazed indignation when he was arrested: he stormed and shouted and argued. Hesitant and embarrassed, his captors took him to a priest, the Dean of Grammont, and begged this ecclesiastic to submit this 'false Dominican spy' to an immediate examination. Father Pire thought he was saved, but he had never been nearer to complete disaster.

The Dean questioned him about the Mass, and as a doctor of theology, Father Pire replied with assurance until he saw that the priest's face was darkening. He was making no impression at all by his replies. At a loss for a moment, he then *suddenly understood! The Dean of Grammont, as a secular priest, was familiar only with the Roman Mass, not the rite in use among the Dominicans and dating from the thirteenth century, which is very different. This led to the reinforcement of the suspicion against him, and since no one was any longer clear about anything, they all shouted and bawled their loudest. Happily there was a local manufacturer among the bystanders, and he intervened in this tragicomedy, changing the ground of the questioning to exact details with which only a true Belgian would be likely to be familiar.*

'I have a son at the college in Melle,' he said suddenly to Father Pire. 'Where is it?'

'Near Ghent! And do you know, my dear sir, a group of pupils from that very college came to make a retreat in my own monastery of La Sarte only a month ago.'

This was confirmed as true, and Father Pire was acquitted amidst a great tumult. He left Grammont and attempted to cross into France as the order issued by the Belgian Government obliged him to try to do.

Two days later he was again arrested, this time by patriots while he was making his way along the canal from Mons to Condé. They took him to a hutted camp for interrogation, and they ended by believing his replies and releasing him. He went off to continue his wanderings, and was joined by other wanderers, a whole Walloon parish going into exile under the leadership of their curé. They formed an alliance on the basis of Father Pire's road map.

I showed them the road, and they supplied me with food! But even these good people glanced at my tonsure uneasily, and I was regarded for the third time as a spy. Only this time they were satisfied with just allowing me to see their suspicions. But, do not think that this sort of thing is only a war-time occurrence. I was arrested at Gratz in

1957 for the very same reason. I was on my travels, and said Mass one morning in the Carmelite church, assisted by the sacristan. He, too, found the Dominican rite not truly Catholic and called in the Austrian police. He had the additional excuse that just previously a *real* false priest, if I may put it that way, had passed through Gratz.

Well, when we had got as far as Doullens the Germans overtook us and it was 'about turn' and back to Belgium. I was the first to return to La Sarte, where I had been appointed steward some months previously.

The monastery was occupied by the Germans, but since they did not recognize my rank as Dominican-parachutist-S.S., I was able to carry on with my duties, which were heavy. I had not only had my lectures to give, but the community to feed.

From the first weeks of the Occupation this became increasingly difficult, especially as we were to see our good Fathers return from France half-starved, having left their cheerful plumpness behind them.

In addition, there were the children of Huy's open-air missions of which I was chaplain. For four years I was a 'Robin Hood' where potatoes, meat, bread, and butter were concerned! Soon, instead of the normal eighty youngsters, we had a thousand banging their spoons on the table, and it did not make the work any easier. But what satisfaction there was in fighting hunger, anaemia, and tuberculosis, and in succeeding. I had innumerable helpers. One of my brother monks, Father Raymond, was promoted lieutenant of my Operation Food. We outdid Homer in a new *Odyssey*: the quest for potatoes. Only Europeans, who have known what war, the Occupation, requisitioning, the disappearance of all foodstuffs and the Black Market really mean, can bear witness that if I jest, I do so to cover a deal of Truth.

In saying so much, he leaves unsaid much more. On the

lapel of his travelling suit various ribbons are ranged: the Médaille de la Reconnaissance Nationale, Médaille de la Ré- *sistance, and the* Croix de Guerre. *During the German Oc- cupation. Father Pire, as chaplain of the Armée Secrète at Hesbaye, used to visit the maquis of this cell of resistance. He arranged stores of medical supplies in the villages, and his motor-cycle was to be heard humming along the roads at night. If he was stopped at a check-point, he would say: 'I am going to see my children.'*

And it was true. He had placed many quarrelsome chil- dren about the countryside, and established many depôts wherever they were: when he said out loud 'children' it was the men of the maquis *he was thinking of.*

He also took charge of a modest information unit, the Service Bayard. *Fifteen agents combed the neighbourhood, and kept watch on Huy's two railway stations, where they counted the trains and tried to find out what they carried and where, for many munitions consignments were carried on this line. One of them, marked out as such and signalled ahead, went on to jump the rails at Marloie in the Ardennes. It is no use pressing Father Pire to tell you about such things as this: he would say no more, probably not so much. Having emerged unscathed from this dangerous period, he seems to think that all he did was of very little importance, and forgets that he would have been no sooner captured than shot.*

And what has he to say of the maquis, *for whom he acted as purveyor with so much courage and patience? He has respect for their self-sacrifice and a certain astonishment, both admiring and sad for the daring and lack of conscience of so many* maquisards. *He had pleurisy, too, caught in a cellar. Four months after the Liberation, Rundstedt's offen- sive ravaged the Ardennes. Father Pire was at Dinant, ill and feverish, with a patch on his left lung. He left his bed to go back to Huy and look out the records of his information*

unit, too good a prize to leave for commandos bent on re-
prisals. He had to drag himself on, as he puts it, from shelter
to shelter in the intervals of alerts, and under the threat of
overhead V1s.

Generally speaking, his was a war against absurdity and
injustice. On his appearance, hunger was banished for the
children, and despair and confusion for the grown-ups.
Having undergone the rule of the Übermenschen, he
dreamed more than ever of helping the weak, the abandoned, and those who were no longer even men. He wanted
to help every lame dog.

Instead, they made him curé of a parish, a shepherd.

CHAPTER SEVEN

Dead Souls

HE HAD TAUGHT for ten years, conscientiously but without enthusiasm, and from time to time putting in a request to his superiors that he be given other duties. As he matured, he found himself a man of action, but a lifeboatman, not a merchant seaman. After the war he made his request yet again. At last, in July 1946, the Provincial of the Order summoned him to Brussels and said: 'I have appointed you curé of La Sarte.'

He was astounded: he who had left the seminary precisely in order not to have a flock, had now been appointed the only Dominican curé in Wallonia! And, as a matter of fact, it is not at all within the province of Dominicans to run parish affairs. Yet, since the monastery church at La Sarte happens to be the spiritual centre of a parish, and belongs to the order, the priest in charge must be a Dominican. However, being in charge of a parish means being subordinate both in administrative affairs and priestly rank to the secular clergy. In this way, Father Pire, now curé of La Sarte, while remaining under the direct authority of his brother monks, passed at the same time under the authority of the Deanery of Huy. Spiritually, he continued to serve the one Master, but in temporal matters he had to serve two. No more of those magnificent tyrants of his soul—his works. There was a duel of duties, open conflict . . .

It is true that he was at first a little put out, but one must not be misled by this. Father Pire has never thought of one form of the Christian apostolate as of a superior or inferior nature compared with others. But he did feel a special call! The limited problems within the peaceful boundaries of a parish seemed to him worthy of the care of the Good Shepherd himself, but he envisaged other, invisibly bounded spheres of action. He undoubtedly hungered after the enormous Parish of the Refugees, the Parish of Destitution— not merely of poverty, and the Parish of the Lost—not the Saved. And he wanted for his parishioners people of all beliefs and every kind of unbelief, the uprooted.

He was a pioneer in search of land to clear: and they gave him a kitchen garden to tend!

But Father Pire had vowed obedience, and he obeyed, giving not merely lip service but all his heart and soul, and bringing his genius for organization to bear on parish affairs. He had certainly jumped into action, but he had fallen, not on the stones he had hoped for, but only reasonably soft sand. Only one thing need cause surprise, however, and that is that he should have 'clericalized' himself. How can I explain this? A Dominican, in the first place by intellectual training, and in the second by the nature of his work, is less closely linked with the times than the curé of a parish who is snowed under with precisely defined tasks. In Belgium they are often caught up in the nation's daily life, even its political and economic affairs.

A curé moves in a limited circle. Polarizing parochial life, he at the same time becomes for those outside the Church the symbol of a clearly defined power, of a course of directed action, and himself sometimes tends to fight not so much exclusively for God, as against men. He is a fighter, or is considered such by his antagonists on the other side, whereas a Dominican preacher, being without pastoral duties, remains on a more detached plane, or at least ap-

pears to do so. Father Pire was sensible of this: contact with unbelievers became more difficult. To them, he appeared to have become a cleric.

The Reverend Father, curé of La Sarte, explored his domain, noting its strongholds and its points of weakness, and drew up a plan. A card index of his parishioners came into being at once, as well as a parish bulletin Ici la Sarte! He drew up a veritable spiritual 'register', and began to hoe his garden of souls, methodically seeing them all, every one, each year. Giving notice of his visits beforehand, he made them—twenty-five a week—from All Saints' Day to Easter. He went from house to house, not forgetting to call again on those who had been away from home the first time . . . or who had not opened their door to him. Not that there were many of the latter: two in the first year, one the second, and after that—none. And in five years . . .

They loved him, and why? Let one of his parishioners explain: 'He helped the poor, distributed clothing, organized decent meals for old people; he listened understandingly to everyone, and created no jealousies. He was seen with the local bigwigs no more often than with anyone else, and, if only he would have talked Walloon, he would have been worshipped.'

But Father Pire did not want to talk Walloon. He got on with making his calls, including the good old lady of ninety who scolded her 'little girl' of sixty-five in front of him, and while carrying on his parochial ministry with all his heart and soul lost his appetite in the process. Visiting takes heavy toll of a curé.

On his first call, at four o'clock, he will be asked: 'You'll take a cup of coffee, won't you Father?' At quarter to five, he is offered an apple. At a quarter past a glass of well-chilled red wine. At six, a little drop of something and a biscuit. Then it starts all over again, only the order being different: apples, coffee, wine, the 'drop of something' . .

Father Pire used to long for a slice of bread and butter to stabilize the mixture, but it never came. Sitting on the edge of their chairs in their Sunday clothes his parishioners would be too overawed to invite him to eat, but never hesitated to press him to drink.

And so, for seven years, from 1946 to 1953, Father Pire, curé of La Sarte, did his duty. Today, presiding at his meals for the old people—they would all want him to play cards afterwards—tomorrow visiting the sick poor, when he would be seen balancing a mattress on his head as he went down the hill. Should anyone leave the parish, that grand little newsletter Ici la Sarte would still pop into his letter-box. Greetings would arrive for everyone on each occasion for rejoicing, for that indefatigable indexer, Father Pire, had made yet another one to cover marriages, births, and anniversaries. Always smiling, attentive, and eager to help, he worked on, and his apostolate continued free of any attempts to constrain belief, glorying only in providing conditions favourable to a change of heart in the agnostic. Because he lived out his faith singleheartedly, others of like mind were drawn to him. Because he had no ulterior motive, they helped him, and because he was himself trusting, they put their faith in him.

In becoming a curé, he did not drop all his other work. On the contrary, the open-air missions, the Family Mutual Aid, the preaching at retreats, and his famous study circles in theology at Huy, Brussels, and Liège all continued.

If this man ever issued a challenge, it was in his determination to preserve the one single right to wear himself out with work and worry.

He was advised to cut down the number of his interests. Even from the Deanery there was a request, and ultimately a command, that he should. Some found fault with him for such 'useless' activities as his running of theology classes. Could there be anything more absurd than giving college *students and Girl Guides ideas, necessarily incomplete and therefore dangerous, of holy doctrine?*

So went the whispers, which were not without malice— that unctuous malice of the ecclesiastical world. But Father Pire was obstinate: the study circles were developed further and their general programme tightened up.

I tried, he said, to establish a regular programme of debates on some topic of living interest, some problem which would enlarge the sympathies of young people. Every month I called on some friend to deal with some particular question.

One day in the January of 1949, I was in urgent need of a speaker, for I had neither a name nor a subject down on the agenda for the Brussels circle for February. The Commissioner of the Girl Guides, Madame Mertens, suggested her brother-in-law, a young American who had worked in the refugee camps. I had never met Ed. Squadrille, as he was called, and of the camps I only knew, as did everyone else, that there was somewhere in Europe a human 'forest' which had been torn up by its roots, and which people were spending millions of dollars planting out again.

Our friend Squadrille arrived: a most agreeable young American, very straightforward, sincere, and kindhearted.

I gave my little talk on theology and then he began speaking about the refugees of the camps. As a former camp commandant at Kufstein in the Austrian Tyrol, where he had been in charge of four thousand souls, he spoke with authority. He had resigned, overcome in part by the death of his little daughter whom he had just laid to rest in Salzburg cemetery, and in part by his feeling of despairing helplessness in his work at the camp. He was convinced that the I.R.O.—International Refugee Organization—regarded the refugee problem primarily as a matter of selection, so that a vast consignment of healthy, virtuous, and efficient emigrants could be delivered to the countries financing the operation.

'They think of it too much as a commercial proposition,' he said, 'and not enough as a question of human beings. There is too much talk of money expended and not enough disquiet about the Hard Core, the twisted in soul and body who will not be emigrating. It has become a well-run emi gration office for able-bodied men and skilled craftsmen. They will pay no attention to the "residue" until they have nothing else to do. That is sound reasoning for the head of a business corporation, but hardly a humane attitude. Yet is it the fault of the I.R.O. or of the practical self-interest of the nations who advance the necessary funds?'

Squadrille was bitter and outspoken, a disillusioned idealist. When he sat down we were all deeply moved, and my little theologians, the Girl Guides, had tears in their eyes. Although we did not know it, our hearts had all been opened in readiness . . .

And so, you see, it was neither the refugees who came to me, nor I who sought out the refugees, went on Father Pire. I was merely a Dominican without a speaker for his theological study-circle, and nothing more. It all just 'happened'. I looked for a speaker, and it was someone to change life's course who came. And Who was it sent him?

Squadrille went away. He had not asked us to solve the problem, but we all felt it impossible to remain indifferent. We had been convinced of that at once on the spot. We said to him, 'What do you think should be done?'

'I don't even know that myself,' he answered slowly. 'Since leaving the camps I have twice tried to arouse the interest of my own country, without achieving any response.'

It was then that we thought of writing letters, just to let

the refugees know that the world had not quite forgotten them.

Squadrille had given me a list of forty-seven names of D.P.s living in Austria. We wrote to them, but I never dreamed that what we slipped into the post-box that day would be so treasured by them, nor that we should receive in return something so heart-rending. I had no special feeling of excitement. My life went on in its usual way, like a stream that insensibly gathers volume as it flows, and at the moment when these letters were despatched I was still not yet a useful, navigable river.

And so the Aid for Displaced Persons germinated by it-self, like a plant: that was the 27th February 1949.

In April Father Pire left for Austria.

'Still with no special feeling of excitement?'

He would say so today and undoubtedly believes it, but then he was possessed by the anguish of what he had learned, and wanted to see for himself so that he could speak to others with the authority of an eyewitness. 'What drove me on,' he told me, 'was the vision of this far-off festering misery.'

There were obstacles to be overcome when he wished to visit the D.P. camps. It was first of all necessary to obtain the permission both of his bishop and the provincial of his order, and when this was given, he had also to have a pass-port, French and Swiss visas, and three separate travel per-mits for the American, British, and French zones of Occu-pied Germany. Finally, there was the special pass for visit-ing the camps, which could only be obtained in Geneva, and even there not without delay.

'Send in your request and then leave at once,' advised his friend Squadrille. 'Wait till it arrives, and you'll never get started.'

This was sound advice and he acted on it. He went on to

visit twenty-four camps, two sanatoria, a home for children, and another for old people: the pass arrived a month
after his return to Belgium, and two months after the date
of his original request.

The administrative machinery, the red-tape of bureaucracy, was the chief enemy of this pilgrim among human
misery. It was not that there had been delay: things had
merely gone through the official channels—quite a simple
matter, as we shall see.

The situation was as follows: someone living at Huy in
Belgium writes to ask the proper authority in Geneva for
a pass. Geneva refers back to Brussels, Brussels refers back
to Namur, and Namur sets an investigation in motion at
Huy. The dossier compiled at Huy was then sent to Namur,
from Namur to Brussels, and from Brussels to Geneva. All
the material has now to be studied and collated, and consideration given above all to the question: 'Why the devil
should anyone, let alone a fellow who is "nobody in particular, not even a journalist", want to go looking round
such unpleasant places.' And then, Geneva grants the permit. And if it is too late? What does time matter in the
world of D.P.s, where all the clocks stopped long ago anyway?

Father Pire slipped away to Austria by way of Switzerland, going off in such a hurry that he left his cloak and hat
behind. He was going to shiver in his white robe in the ice-
cold wind of that Danubian spring.

On his first arrival in Linz he fell in with a smartly uni-
formed I.R.O. staff officer taking a midday aperitif at the
Hotel Prielmayerhof. A good enough fellow, like the rest of
his kind, but with the outlook of an occupying power: a
nice little villa near the camp, a domestic staff chosen from
among the D.P.s, and a few more to wash the car down and
do the odd jobs.

Good enough fellows and not so underpaid: at this period

an American assistant social worker received 420 dollars a month, plus an overseas allowance. Something of a contrast with the level of wages in Austria, where a certificated nurse earned 550 schillings a month, a secretary 470 schillings, and a black-coated official 1,000 to 1,200 schillings, and where the purchasing power of 25 schillings was the same as that of one dollar. In effect, therefore, the nurse secretary and official were earning 22, 19, and 40 dollars a month. As a costume or a pair of shoes cost 12 dollars and a dinner one dollar, the economic situation and the state of local morale can be imagined. While the American spent his money like a wealthy tourist, and the too-trusting British got their jeeps driven for them by former Luftwaffe parachutists, and the French took seriously and sternly to their role of 're-educating' the occupied country, the Austrians spent their time marvelling at their own poverty. With what trace of altruism their own rationing difficulties left them, they allowed what they could to the Volks Deutsch, the members of German minorities who had lived before the war beyond the Danube. During the war these people had been incorporated—for the most part willingly —into the Greater Reich as additional manpower for industry, agriculture, and the army. They were considered by the occupation powers of 1949 as 'collaborators', and stagnated miserably in camps, on minimum American aid. The Austrians took pity on them and reserved for them what little work there was to spare, but the Volks Deutsch had only one real hope—the promise that they would be settled somewhere in Germany. Germany was later to keep that promise.

Father Pire took the plunge into the strange system of classifying human beings like animals. He learned to distinguish the V.D. from the D.P.—the Volks Deutsch from the Displaced Persons, and mastered the further distinction between good and bad D.P.s. The good D.P. had been able to

supply the occupying authorities with proof that during
the war he had been anti-Hitler, or a conscientious objec-
tor, or even a member of the underground resistance. The
bad D.P. was the man with no proof, and therefore with no
'Eligibility'. He was not even 'eligible', let alone one of the
'Chosen'.

Eligibility was granted to those D.P.s who had not col-
laborated with the Germans. These D.P.s swarmed every-
where, since the Allied administration showed a merciful
blindness, living in camps and bombed buildings. The non-
eligible D.P.s were less numerous, and this alone should
have made it clear to every simple soul that between 1939
and 1945 half the German population and all her allies
secretly worshipped Churchill, Eisenhower, and De
Gaulle!

These non-eligible D.P.s were sternly treated: they lived
in bombed buildings and camps . . . They were scorned, and
received the supreme mark of scorn: they were not in-
cluded in the official statistics!

Coming from the East, the Baltic countries, Poland,
Rumania, the Ukraine, Czechoslovakia, Yugoslavia—the
D.P.s dreamed only of getting away to the West. In 1949
there were 750,000 eligible D.P.s hoping for an I.R.O. pass-
port, a chance to emigrate, food to eat, clothing to wear.
And in the hutted camps they did odd jobs as they waited,
nothing more. The Settlement Scheme, as it was called,
meant emigration. The machinery involved was excellent,
and we may as well reproduce here what Father Pire said of
it in the brochure he published on his return from the
camps.

'At the moment the Settlement Scheme works well. The
consuls and missions from the various interested countries
visit the camps, notify the number of vacant places, and
choose the people they want.

'Alas, governments are more head than heart. They make

their choice for the Settlement Scheme as a dealer judges horses.

'The standards of health, strength, and skill by which they are guided are often pitiless, compassion and humanitarian feeling seldom entering into the matter, so that little by little those remaining in the camps are reduced to what the Americans have called the Hard Core. This residue consists of the very old, who have no relatives overseas, the very ill, those who have suffered the loss of a limb, and the many, many families who have been deprived of the bread-winner. The old people with no family and the incurable invalids are in a hopeless position.'

One can add to the Hard Core also the intellectual D.P.s.
In 1949 their number was still overwhelming, Russian émigrés of 1917 and Hungarians predominating. Let them be judges, lawyers, scholars, university professors, or engineers, if they were old or ill the same simple remedy applied. Off with them into the ranks of the Hard Core! If they were still young and in good health, these wretched people had better not persist in wanting to emigrate in the role of intellectuals. Intellectuals have no commercial value as exports. If they really wanted to emigrate, their best chance was to put themselves down as manual workers, and so many called themselves gardeners. If an old up-rooted doctor was no longer thought capable of attending to the sick, he would tend flower-beds ...

There were still the students. Their position in 1949 was difficult, but the governments set to work pretty efficiently to solve this problem, notably by granting scholarships to the U.S.A. A fine, disinterested action, or merely a good investment? In fact, every student is a source of future productivity.

Shocking? Not at all. Simply an automatic process at

work. It was not individual people who were responsible, and we know that in the years since 1949, hundreds of thousands, even millions, of refugees have been enabled to find some sort of normal life again thanks to those hundreds of millions of dollars. But now, as in 1949, the Hard Core exists.

This is not because no one has attempted to do anything about it, but as soon as one tries to empty the 'machine' fom the bottom, it refills from the top. We must not forget that in the intervening years certain countries of the East have re-entered the refugee-manufacturing business, and have not merely saturated the market, but reached the point of over-production.

On 3rd November 1958 the High Commissioner for refugees announced that 160,000 refugees still remained to be rescued, 40,000 of them living in the camps. What percentage of them belong to the Hard Core? We are only likely to know that after the cream has been skimmed off this milk of suffering, for the methods of selection are unchanged. At the top of the list in the criteria of judgement there still stand: freedom from tuberculosis, a full complement of teeth, and well-developed biceps.

In this mechanized system, the punched cards still had no additional space to be filled in by the investigator under the heading of 'Brotherly Love'.

In 1959 certain international bodies were waking up. Campaigns were being launched: 'Not a single D.P. in 1960, no more Hard Core.' Yet they still exist, do they not? There are still plenty of problems to solve.

It is all right! The I.R.O. officials can count on a few more pleasant days, and on a few more delightful week-ends in the Tyrol where the Alpine slopes are so good for skiing. No! You cannot do good simply by tapping on a typewriter or calculating physical effort according to a tariff. You cannot be kindly and humane through official channels. It takes

*three months' endurance of life in the huts to acquire the
necessary minimum of experience.*

*How many among the high officials who have busied
themselves for years in this precious business of sorting
and clearing have spent even a full twenty-four hours in
camp?*

*But these are only the black beads of the rosary, let us
have a look at the white ones. In spite of the stifling bureaucracy which had sometimes caused excellent plans and
projects to be thwarted or neglected, how much splendid
devotion had been shown! The I.R.O. had established efficient social services: inquiry into hopeless cases, welfare,
technical training courses, medical care. There were also
the Voluntary Societies, mainly run by the English and
Americans, which had distributed immense sums, the Protestant societies sometimes giving up to 40 per cent. of their
aid to Catholic and Orthodox D.P.s. The American dioceses
had given very largely to the work of rescue.*

*To sum up, the greater part of the civilized world put up
funds when necessary, but those figures still stand. At the
time when Father Pire was going from camp to camp increasingly depressed—increasingly encouraged, too, for
this fisher of souls and men of goodwill found a few 'real
bricks', as he would call them, everywhere—at this very
time when he was making his pilgrimage, 160,000 'insoluble' cases were dragging out a miserable existence in the
hutted cities. This is confirmed by a report on the refugee
situation issued by the Director-General of the I.R.O. from
Geneva, and dated 29th October 1949. As for the results
obtained by attempting to find a refuge for members of the
Hard Core in Western countries, these were pitifully inade-
quate: 50 blind people sent to Norway, 10 old people to
Holland, and 75 more to Belgium. Out of 166,000 so-called
insoluble cases, just 35 had been solved. And how many of
the others among that 160,000 still remain insoluble cases?*

No one can say. Although 'hard core' cases sometimes cling to life, they would in any case probably not be the same ones as in 1949, for death itself does a merciful share in the work of reclassification.

We do, however, know this: according to Auguste Lindt, United Nations High Commissioner for refugees, there were still twenty-five thousand D.P.s in the camps of Austria, Germany, Greece, and Italy on the 30th April 1959. Five thousand three hundred D.P.s had left the camps between 1st January and 30th April of that year, thanks to the programme of evacuation planned for World Refugee Year. Belgium had decided to take over the social reintegration of three thousand refugees, either by assisting them to emigrate, though not necessarily to Belgium, or by helping them to settle wherever they were. The Belgian Committee for World Refugee Year made it clear at the end of June that they would seek 'a humane solution for every individual case, taking into account both the preferences expressed by each refugee and the practical possibilities open to him'. The situation would seem, on the whole, to have improved: the 'humane solution' is an accepted principle. But in 1949 there were 160,000 insoluble cases, and this is what Father Pire first discovered for himself and then proclaimed to the world.

CHAPTER EIGHT

The Uprooted

FATHER, *what were you going to do in the Austrian camps?*

I wanted to see the Hard Core. Just that. I was driven to plod on from hutted camp to hutted camp by a kind of melancholy desire to know the worst. Fifty thousand children were then living there, on potatoes and American tinned food. Twenty thousand of them had been born out of wedlock, but who could be surprised at that? Who would marry D.P.s? If an Austrian girl ventured it, she was herself officially classed as a D.P. On the other hand, if an Austrian man married a D.P., she took his Austrian nationality. So, they either had children without marrying, or else married, not to have children, but to get a passage to America! Marriage, in either case, entitled them to emigrate free of charge. Of course, the powers that be would never have dared to forbid D.P.s to marry. Instead, the Austrian civil authorities merely required that their papers be in order. And would a D.P. fiancé risk going back to the country from which he had fled, just in order to get them? Of course not. The practical-minded Americans, on the other hand, simply announced that they would no longer subsidize passages in such cases, since so many of the couples divorced as soon as they reached the U.S.A. At once the marriages ceased, but not the births.

That is only an example, there were a thousand such aspects to being a D.P. It just shows the fantastic state of the world into which I had come—a fourth dimension of the human mind.

I came across camps where religious and social ranks were still respected, where one section was given over to the Russian nobility, another to the black marketeers, another to pig-keepers . . . Yet they had one thing in common, they were beggars all.

And these camps we are talking about, were they fenced with barbed wire, subject to strict supervision, hemmed in with Verboten *notices?*

No, it was worse than that : the material means of existence were assured. Supplies might be scanty, but they arrived regularly every day. Lodging, food, and coal, the necessities of life, were provided for these castaways, and the D.P. allowed himself to drift, secure in his maintenance ration. No one was a prisoner, except of his own apathy, listlessness, or despair.

What did they tell you on your visits to the huts?

Sometimes, in the night, I still can hear those whispered confidences, and the tragedy of them resounds in my memory like the strokes of an axe.

He took from a chest in his office the first notebook he had kept on his journeys and read out his notes, the dreadful diagnoses which were purely factual, but were sad as a lament.

Forty people of both sexes living in one room, thirty-three feet by thirteen, with sixteen panes of glass in the windows and an equal number blocked with cardboard. They are entitled to 2 lbs. of coal per person per day.

An old granny of sixty-seven, with her daughter and grand-children aged ten, seven and three. The son-in-law disappeared four years ago.

Two hundred Poles with T.B. They are not incurable, but need rest and care to fit them for work.

Three sisters, the youngest seventy-one.

An old lady of eighty all by herself.

A widow with six children.

One hundred and twenty tuberculosis patients in a sana-torium, twenty of them without shirts. T.B. patients get an extra ration of milk of under half a pint a day.

Forty people in a bombed house with no doors or windows, and paying the Austrians a very high rent.

A father and his six children.

A young woman, a patient in the sanatorium for a year, has a husband in the camp : he has lost both arms.

One hundred and fifty old people over sixty.

Husband, wife and six children : the husband and two of the children having T.B.

Four old men, one ninety-two, living together.

Four young children, their father killed in the war and their mother now in hospital.

An old doctor, formerly a university professor.

A seventy-year-old Professor of Civil Law, with his deaf-mute daughter, aged thirty.

Two lonely and ill old ladies of over seventy.

Father Pire stopped reading and there was a long silence while I gathered courage to play devil's advocate.

But these are the especially sad cases you are telling me about. Were there so very many?

Had there been only one, it would have been not a single spot of rain, but a drop of scalding water, said Father Pire. And it was a downpour ! Leaving out of account those D.P.s with no chance of emigrating because they were a poor economic proposition, and including only old people without families and incurable invalids—and only the most unfortunate even of these—I arrived at a percentage of 3·5: that is to say, two thousand of the D.P.s in Austria, and twenty thousand from the whole herd. Yes, 'herd' is the right word.

After all, these cases were *real*, actually *existed*. I had discovered a few of them. But it was just the fact that their being so was known, officially admitted, and filed away in the dossiers of the administration under the heading 'Nothing to be Done'; just this wretched business of shelving the whole matter, that appalled me.

Was it also true, though, that the officials in charge of the refugees showed goodwill, kindness, keenness to help, and a sense of social responsibility?

Undoubtedly. I met some wonderful people, but hampered by red tape and above all by their orders. What could they hope to do about the problem of the Hard Core when they kept on receiving from these wealthy nations such terribly precise instructions in the matter of selection? When a government might demand, for example, that they send two hundred shoemakers? It was fatally inevitable that they should end by substituting in their own minds the category: 'Person-able-to-make-shoes' for the real and worth while: 'So-and-so, a married man and father of a child.'

But, it was not only the sight of misery condemned as irremediable which troubled me. What cut me to the quick in the D.P. camps of 1949 was the almost absolute lack of the boundless compassion of glowing Christian feeling.

Some benefactors would only concern themselves with Protestants, or with those of the Greek Orthodox or Catholic faith. Others, only with Hungarian Catholics or Polish Catholics. Each had his own circle of clients. But misfortune had touched all D.P.s making each worthy of interest, and for Christians they *had to be* worthy of interest simply because they were men and brothers. This benevolence only inside certain limits, this absence of the true face of Christ, caused me almost physical pain. Would he have demanded on entering a camp : 'Are you Catholics ?' The whole Gospel says otherwise.

Sometimes in those hours he spent talking to me, the steep, echoing staircase that leads up to his office would creak under his secretary's tread. She was bringing up a dinner which he would swallow down in ten minutes. When at Huy he spends all day here from eight in the morning until eight in the evening: sometimes he comes earlier in the morning, and just to make up for it, stays later in the evening! Then he goes back up to the monastery, and next day, after celebrating Mass, comes down again to begin all over again. No one counts his mail any more: they just weigh it.

Work and concentrated thought during these years have taken their toll, and physically he is half the man he was.

'Only prayer enables me to pull myself together.'

He said it with a smile, and went on with his story.

I have described to you the strange country and yet stranger people among whom I suddenly found myself. It was like a prolonged nightmare. You must sometimes have watched tramps, the way they have of walking aimlessly on ? But at least they keep going ahead, guided by the whimsical impulse of their own will. In the camps I met tramps by the thousand, but they were just sitting still or walking in circles, captives of their own discouragement and feeling of uselessness. They were free, but the world was against them. Both Austrians and Germans treated them harshly till 1948, impelled by memories of the war, the bitterness born of hunger and defeat, and to some degree by communist propaganda which never ceased referring to them as bandits. The D.P.s were familiar with military administration and receiving contradictory instructions. The Americans tended to dissuade them from mingling with the German population, saying, 'What's the good? You'll be leaving soon.' The French rather favoured integration. The local authorities were not in favour of anything. But I hesitate to give you too many details. For the tragedy of the D.P.s has a truly diabolical quality! It is like a kaleidoscope in that a single movement on the part of the viewer changes the whole pattern. One could give two completely objective accounts of life as lived by the D.P.s: one frightful, the other a completely rosy picture, the difference arising purely from the contrasts in the places where they happened to be, the living conditions, and their states of mind.

Some D.P. communities were very well housed, and the families had succeeded in rebuilding comfortable enough nests for themselves. But a few miles further on, you came back to wooden shacks, Nissen huts, bombed houses, and converted 'bunkers'.

In one place the D.P.s would have inherited a hutted camp which had been inhabited successively by 'anti-social' Germans put out of the way by Hitler; then by French prisoners-of-war; then by evacuee Germans. In another they would be lodged in gloomy barracks, where the rooms had been divided off into separate quarters by wooden partitions. Once there, let them shift for themselves, let them squat there ten or twenty years! Let them devour each other and bark at the heels of anyone making his way into their infernal circle!

Yet other D.P.s would be living in the metal tubes invented by the Anglo-Saxon race—Nissen huts, those 'Little tunnels to let'. And the most unfortunate of all would be buried in the enormous shelters used by the Germans during the air raids, with some ten feet of concrete between themselves and daylight! Even the air had to be pumped down by ventilators. I saw one of these foul places at Mannheim. The electric light, necessary for twenty-four hours out of twenty-four, was paid for by the municipality, but the cost of keeping the ventilators going fell on the D.P.s. They were poor, and so the ventilators functioned only for two hours in twenty-four.

It was indeed diabolical, and the more so because at that very moment in another part of Germany the authorities had requisitioned for the D.P.s a whole village which had formerly been made over by the Third Reich to munition workers: 306 houses, two hospitals, two schools, a home for old people, a kindergarten, a canteen, and twenty shops.

And so, those who give a favourable and unfavourable diagnosis of the D.P. situation will both for ever have right on their side.

Father Pire closed his eyes a moment and then, with a start, went on:

Do not forget that it is the Hard Core I am telling you about! Above all, never forget that! I have just been thinking of all those D.P.s who have passed through the sieves of the nations, and have emigrated and are for the most part happy, and even grateful. How many of them? A million, two million? I want you to record what an immense achievement this has been, but I want you to add immediately afterwards that every human being, even those of the Hard Core, is of infinite worth, and deserves respect and loving-kindness, firstly because he is a human being, secondly because he is considered 'useless', and finally because he is unfortunate. This is what international bureaucracy has

forgotten, and that is the cause of which I have made myself the advocate—that of the last chance. I do not want to
burden with examples the unknown friends who may perhaps read this book, but I still must try to make them understand what being a D.P. means, and what the Hard Core of
1949 was like. Why was it that these uprooted people had
gradually become disorientated and dehumanized? Never
previously asocial, why had they now become so?

He dived once more into his chests, bringing out docu-
ments which he held out to me. They described with terse
precision a series of human tragedies, the lives of humble
people . . . Will these poor wretches ever find a Plutarch to
immortalize their story?

The M. family fled from their native country in 1944. There
were originally five children, four sons and a daughter, but the
youngest son had been carried off by partisans during the family
exodus, and the parents were for many years completely in
ignorance of what had become of him. They then learned that
the unfortunate young man was imprisoned, and though he
was subsequently released his efforts to rejoin them were fruit-
less. At first the rest of the family stayed in various Austrian
camps, but in 1947 the mother fell ill and died, and in the same
year the eldest son became seriously affected by sciatica, and is
now at the age of twenty-eight still incapable of working. The
father is so asthmatic that he, too, can no longer work. The two
other sons emigrated to the U.S.A. in 1951, and the daughter
could have gone with them, but she stayed to look after her
invalid father and brother and is the only breadwinner of the
family, for the two brothers had no luck in the States. A series
of accidents at work prevented them for months from earning
a living, and they have still been unable to make any contribu-
tion to the support of the invalids. Consequently the whole
burden rests on the sister who wears herself out to earn a little
money during the day, and must busy herself with housework
and the care of the invalids when she comes home in the
evening.

Here we have the case of two Lithuanians, brothers aged

forty-four and thirty-seven. Good kindly men, uneducated and simple-hearted, but religious and decent. The younger, a deaf-mute, has a paralysed left hand. The elder, who has a serious impediment of speech, would not emigrate with the rest of the family because he did not want to leave behind alone the deaf-mute who had been denied an emigration permit. Their way of life is primitive and they hardly ever sit down to a cooked meal. A little slow and deliberate in manner, they are nevertheless fundamentally good men.

Here is what a D.P. wrote who had just left a sanatorium after a very lengthy stay :
'I live in the old military barracks. The rooms are deplorable. I shall never forget the day when I first set foot here. I had just come from the sanatorium and I had never seen such a dreadful place.
'It is a new world for me, and what a world! The people round me are invalids, cripples, mental defectives and criminals —nine of us to a room with no furniture. All I have is a bed and my belongings are just stowed away beneath it.'

Here is a Polish family consisting of father, forty-one and suffering from T.B., mother aged thirty-six, a little boy of three, also tuberculous, and his one-year-old sister. The husband is by profession a photographer.
The couple had just married in Poland in 1939 and before their marriage had lived in good middle-class style. From 1939 to 1943 they were imprisoned at J. They were then transferred to Sk., and in 1944 to Sz. In January 1945, although the wife was freed, the husband was interned in Buchenwald. Their first child had been born in Poland, and the mother, having foreseen her own arrest, entrusted him to some peasants whom she knew : she reclaimed him on her release, but the child died soon after their entry into Germany. The husband was set free at A. later in 1945.
After spells in a number of D.P. camps the family arrived in 1951 at F. The husband has been undergoing treatment since January 1952 at the sanatorium at G.

Father, this is terrible . . .

I have been living with this sort of thing ten years. I am

still not hardened to it, and never wish to be. Besides, such wretchedness always has some new aspect to show. Misfortune has a macabre, picturesque element, sometimes a weird humour in its monotony. Listen to this classic case-history, that of a D.P. who thought to escape, but when he jumped over the fence he found it was only the first obstacle in a steeplechase. Once on the run, he must take fence after fence, and they whip him up from behind so that he may jump better and faster. Naturally the course is a circular one. Just listen !

He read me a letter:

22nd June 1956.

Dear Sir,

Since I am at the moment being held in Belgium on a charge of 'illegal residence' and find myself classified as a 'stateless person', I ask your kind assistance in obtaining the help I need.

I have declared in a statement to the examining magistrate of the Court of Summary Jurisdiction at G. that I was born at C. in [such-and-such a country] on the 24th November 1929, and lived in the district until 1945. The French people with whom I lodged were shot by the Germans in 1944, and in the next year I was deported from my country to Austria. After a few weeks, this country in its turn deported me to Switzerland, and I was interned in a camp near Berne until 1949, when I was deported to France. I stayed in Paris for almost a year, and then entered the Hôpital de la Pitié (Boulevard de l'Hôpital) for a stomach operation. I underwent a prolonged convalescence at the Red Cross Centre, 107 quai de Valmy, Paris Xe, then in 1952 was again sent to Switzerland where I was interned at Geneva until 1954, when I was sent to Germany until the January of 1955. Once more deported, this time to Holland, I stayed in Amsterdam at the disposal of the aliens' section of the Police Department until September of that year, was then sent back to Belgium, and in December to France, which in February 1956 again returned me to Belgium. By May I had been sent to Holland, which sent me back to Belgium, which sent me on to France, which finally, on 19th June, sent me back to Belgium. That is my story. Knowing that you are working for stateless persons, I beg you to find me some fixed place of residence. I have committed no crimes, no thefts.

Signed I. R.

Letting the letter fall on the table, Father Pire looked across at me, and in some discouragement I ventured to ask: What happened to him, this hunted wretch?

I was able to catch him, as it were, on the wing and he is now in a home run by the Aid for Displaced Persons at Braine-le-Comte in Belgium. Of course, there had to be another inquiry, yet one more! The poor man had told the truth, but it was not the whole truth.

Ah, so there was still something else to be told!

Yes, one of those things that even D.P.s do not invent. He was maimed, having only one arm, and during his stay in Switzerland he had acted as guinea-pig to the medical unit of a big international organization. He tried out artificial limbs for them. Before he was expelled the country, they were careful to remove the artificial arm that he was using that day.

---◆---

CHAPTER NINE

But what is a D.P.?

THERE WAS ONCE *a kindly woman at Ghent in Belgium, the mother of three children, who had heard of the distress suffered by D.P.s and knew that a Dominican at Huy was working for these outcasts. She wrote to him: 'Give me the name and address of a mother with several children and I will try to befriend them.'*

The Aid for Displaced Persons organization gave her a name and address, that of Madame Z. at Trieste, a girl-mother with three children. The kind woman of Ghent became their 'godmother' and exchanged many letters with her protégés, sending them parcels, money, and much loving-kindness.

One of the three children of the D.P. at Trieste was a little boy of ten who sent his godmother in Ghent, happy little letters. All seemed going well until, one day, a letter arrived which thoroughly upset her:

Dear Godmother,

I am just writing a few words to let you know that I am in very bad health, and—sad, sad news—my studies, my schooling and my hopes of becoming a priest must all come to an end. There seems no doubt that I am not much longer for this world . . . I want to live, but the camp has robbed me of the chance . . .

Some days later another letter arrived:

My very dear Godmother,

As long as I live I shall still write to you. When I am gone my brother will write, for Mummy cries a lot because of me and her sight is failing. There seems no doubt that she will never recover it as long as she lives ...

One suffering from tuberculosis and the other blind! The poor godmother consulted Father Pire. How could they deal most quickly and effectively with these new misfortunes. The Aid for Displaced Persons organization gave the address of their Liaison Service at Trieste who took immediate action and reported to Ghent:

We have long been familiar with the case of Madame Z. She is certainly not blind and her little boy does not have T.B. Everything the child has written is untrue, and those who know Madame Z. were unanimous in thinking that it was she who dictated the letters to her little son, who is himself a very good, well-behaved boy. When questioned on the subject, she unhesitatingly and unashamedly admitted as much, and when she was asked how she dared to push her own child into committing such an action, she calmly shrugged her shoulders and said with indifference: 'So what! If those people over there in Belgium don't like it, they can do the other thing.' She undoubtedly hoped to get substantially increased gifts by these lies, and the case is all the more tragic in that the children are really very nice. The mother pays them very little attention.

At once relieved and terribly disappointed the godmother away in Ghent wondered what to do—give up, or persevere? But it was the moral problem that troubled her most. Without any ulterior motive, she had wanted to do good, and her loving-kindness had met only with duplicity. Why? Even as she asked herself these questions, she looked at her own children, forget the hurt in the thought of those three other children in Trieste, and continued her help.

Four years later she sat down one day to write to Father Pire:

Very Reverend Father,

I am so happy to tell you that my god-daughter Madame Z. and her children, in whom I have taken such an interest these past four years, have been in England since the end of June. Madame Z. is working as a hospital nurse, and the children are at a convent school. Siegfried, the eldest who is now thirteen, is always the one to write to me. He is a charming boy and I am deeply attached to him, but I am writing chiefly to tell you of the touching gesture my godchildren have made. They have sent me a five dollar bill with a note saying: 'We will send more when we have it, because we will never forget the help you have been.'

I write to them still, and although they no longer need help, I send them a little present from time to time to maintain the links forged between us in the time of their distress. Later, I hope they may come and see me . . .

This story Father Pire told me, with its mingling of light and shade, was one chosen from thousands. The day before, after we had discussed the Hard Core for hours, I had said to him:

Father, we have only skirted the problem, I feel myself confronted by a closed world, a sort of swarming of helpless bees! I can see the outline of the Hard Core, but I cannot see beyond that, it remains a kind of sociological abstraction. Who are the people who make up the Hard Core, who are these human beings crushed by misfortune? I can see the D.P.s, but I cannot see a D.P.: what is it that makes someone a D.P.?

What he had just told me, had been the beginning of his reply. Just a prelude . . .

For three years, he said, when I asked myself that same question, I thought I knew the answer. A D.P. was a human being who had lost his country, and all that was needed to stop his being one, was to give him another. But during those three years I decided myself, and ten years of subsequent experience have confirmed the lesson of my initial error: you cannot give a man a new country. All you can do is just make it possible for him to dream free from care of the old.

The D.P., this man uprooted from his native soil, torn from his social setting, and cowed by want and the kind of regulation ill-luck that attends all state aid, has been thrust into an unreal world. He has been taken out of his own time and projected into this super-neolithic present which we may call 'The Age of Hutments', and he begins to acquire a special sort of mentality. His personality disintegrates to a larger or smaller degree, according to his level of intelligence and strength of will, and becomes merged in the mentality common to all D.P.s.

A dull new world takes shape, a realm of shadows. For three years I deceived myself, I mistook the refugee for a pauper. But 'poverty' is not the word to describe his misfortune, the refugee is primarily someone who has been uprooted and who drifts between the East from which he has fled and the West which very often will not admit him unless he has retained his muscular strength. Living for long years in a camp or an old barracks, he grows bitter. I have often given the definition of a D.P. as: 'A stateless person, spiritless and hopeless.'

A stateless person . . . Notice the negative words one uses in talking about him: stateless, heimatlos, auslander, residue, hard core, Europe's surplus.

Spiritless and hopeless: uprooting a human being involves for him the worst of all misfortunes, the total loss of belief in human comradeship. That is why so many refugees are embittered, take to drink to drown their sorrow, and are so often lacking in concern for personal appearance, ability to manage their affairs, and willingness to work. It is not laziness but a canker of the soul. They will not face up to reality, dreaming either of their lost country or of a future impossible to attain. At Frankfort

one day a highly intelligent Orthodox priest said to me:
'They are sitting on their luggage in the station, and have
waited a dozen or more years for a train that will never
arrive.' And he added: 'The worst of it is not that they
have their luggage—their memories of their beloved native
lands—but that they are sitting on it—living in the past
rather than using the present to build up a new life.'

Mind you, no one can build a life by himself, let alone
rebuild one. As Lord Baden-Powell said: 'Self-confidence
is born of others' confidence in us.' The refugee has lost his
self-confidence, and it is up to us to give it back to him.
When we laid the foundation-stone of our fifth European
Village, Village Albert Schweitzer, in a wonderful atmosphere of friendly co-operation, the Chief Minister of the
Saar said:

'It is not enough to give a stateless person a new house
and a weekly wage. He will only be able to take up a new
and normal life if he feels around him true human devotion, if he knows that others approach him with complete
confidence, if self-respect, a sense of independence and the
assurance of having equal rights with others, revive within
him. The refugee needs the friendship of all those whom
he will be living among.'

The Minister was very right, but this ideal is difficult to
attain, not merely because of unco-operativeness on the
part of the refugees, but because of the prejudices we all
have against them.

You can take it from me that there is much more hatred
of foreigners in the world than anyone would imagine! I
will tell you about it when I explain the how and why of
my founding of the European Villages. Do you now know
what a D.P. is? A man without hope, suspicious of everything, even of the good people try to do for him.

Not that they are all like that. I have met with gratitude
and integrity. I have watched many lovely flowers come

into bloom, but how many other plants have withered! Oh, I could overwhelm you with my 'white' dossiers, putting before you a D.P. Universe right-thinking, dazed with happiness, praying ceaselessly for their benefactors. I could also spread open my 'black' dossiers, showing you failures, frauds, breaches of trust, the disillusion of people with feeling hearts, the completely cold forgetfulness shown by those who had been helped. But all that would give no true picture of the D.P., poised as he is between injustice and ingenuousness! That is why I told you the story of the girl-mother of Trieste and the godmother of Ghent, sublime in her simplicity. When a kind heart does a good action and is mocked for it, what happens? The truly good and kind *persists*. Yes, goes on doing good, even without hope or result achieved, for not every story ends as happily as that of Trieste.

Perseverance is the watchword of my life, though I am myself far from sublime. What I undertake, I persevere in, purely for the sake of Good, of Goodness for itself alone. People do not always understand me, sometimes even opposing this conception from ancient and deep conviction, such as their belief in a utilitarian apostolate and of a charity which tends to regard conversion as the proper exchange for a kind act.

One very old man, a worthy man in every way, said to me once:

'How many old people have you in your homes?'

'Two hundred.'

'What do you do for them?'

'Feed them . . .'

'How many have you "brought in" so far?'

He was using an old missionary expression: 'to bring in to God, to Holy Church.'

'None.'

'Then, what is *the use* of it?' He flung at me.

'To feed them . . . When one gathers in a human being who is wretched, the act of feeding him is its own justification. One does not feed in order to convert . . .'

He broke off for a moment, deeply moved, but at the same time an absolute certainty shone in his eyes. He went on:

But do not make any mistake! There is no need to see me as bereft of my Catholic faith, my role as a priest!

If you say to me: 'Is it a matter of indifference to you whether a soul possesses or does not possess integral Truth?' I answer: 'No.'

I do not set myself apart from the traditional attitude of believers in the matter of the end to be attained, but their methods are not mine.

What is your way, Father?

Mine stems from the principle: 'The more you seek, the less you find.' I believe simply in the force of example and the power of prayer and secret sacrifice. I believe in the virtue of suffering offered to God without anyone's knowledge. For example . . .

He thought for a moment before going on:

Do you know of the little Sisters of Foucauld? They live among the natives in Africa, in just the same way and amid the same poverty, making their homes in the same sort of shacks and eating the same food. They look after the children and the sick, and cultivate their own little patch of cassava. There they stay, lost in the great spaces, isolated in a desert of humanity. And what are they doing? They are in readiness as examples, they are *example incarnate*, and this is what I am trying to do in my own small way, achieve catalysis, not conversion. *In actual fact, no one ever makes a convert, only God can do that!* We are only God's crystals. His light shines through us to fall on others. All we can do is polish the glass, so that the ray shall shine through brightly.

Father, the D.P.s have taken us a long way . . .

A long way indeed! But it is always the same when talking of them. The story of their distress awakes one's conscience, and soon one no longer looks at them but into oneself.

Since we have touched on the religious problem, can you clear up a point? No man of goodwill who carried on his work under the public eye is ever free from criticism. People never seem able to admit that a priest can love his neighbour without attempting to make converts. What do you say to that?

Nothing! I have just explained myself from a spiritual viewpoint. In practice I carry on my work with never a thought as to whether I should favour a Catholic D.P. because he happens to be of my religion. There is only one Catholic in my Old People's Home at Antwerp, not one here at Huy, and in my home at Esneux, maybe three or four. The same applies to my European villages. Chance or Providence, people can take the word they prefer, but I never make a deliberate choice one way or the other. I am neither one of those priests who like to hear themselves described as 'liberals', nor am I among those to whom such men are anathema.

In the camps I have seen Orthodox priests made hard, cruel, and merciless by their too-intense patriotism, and I have seen a Polish Catholic priest unwilling to give a Christmas parcel to a mother because she had sent her child to a German kindergarten. He was not acting as a priest but as a Pole. And are the camps really the ideal place for starting discussions on Faith?

When I listen to that sort of thing, I am reminded of prisoners discussing liberty inside a gaol. I believe that religious problems should not be put to the down-trodden. Pasteur said: 'One doesn't ask a person in distress: What is your country? What is your religion? One says: You are suffering that is enough for me, and I will help you.' I could not put it better than that myself, and I have never done better.

I know: the road I have chosen is narrow and difficult. Since I have always opposed classification of any kind, I have evidently been myself 'classified'. From the beginning . . .

Some Catholics in my own country have labelled me 'neutral', and in the eyes of some that is a severe criticism. Neutral, because I have no love for narrowness of soul! On the religious plane this is the narrowest of all narrow-mindedness. Religion is a matter of love not caste.

Non-believers, or those of other faiths, have often declared that I was 'committed', simply because I was a Dominican and a priest. Just judging by the colour of my habit!

Since I am neither neutral nor committed, I have been walking these last ten years along the ridge-tiles of the roof, as it were.

And what are you really?

I place myself humbly at the disposal of God, that through me he may bring to pass good.

Light through transparence, Father . . .

CHAPTER TEN

———————————◆———————————

The Electric Thrill

BY THE END OF 1949 *Father Pire had marshalled a thousand sponsors, and the list of forty-seven names from the Tyrolean camp at Kufstein supplied by Ed. Squadrille had been added to. The first to offer themselves as 'godmothers' had been the Girl-Guide theologians. Then their families, friends, and more distant relatives had been drawn in—a real round-up!*

The 'Sponsorship Service' imperceptibly took shape, and grew steadily bigger, like a plant thrusting towards the light. Above all, sponsorship is a form of aid for the mind and spirit: it gives confidence and courage, brings from far away a smile and friendly handclasp—acts like an electric thrill. Naturally, material aid—parcels, money—follows, but it is not the same as the official 'hand-out'. Here, the gift is a personal matter. The fact that there were in 1960 some eighteen thousand sponsors shows that the idea met a deep need. People of twenty different nationalities are corresponding with D.P.s, the refugee writing in his own tongue and the sponsor replying in French, English, or German.

Kindly translators lend their services to both sides, and in 60 per cent. of the cases the interchange of letters is a success and is continued. The aim is to use the correspondence constructively. In one case a 'godfather' or 'godmother' will pay for a typewriter, so that a widow with young chil-

dren *may work at home: in another a course of treatment*
may be offered to an invalid, or a bicycle to a worker who
has to reach his factory on foot. In yet another instance, a
boy or girl may be assisted to study so that after their un-
happy childhood in the camps, they may become more
fully integrated in some sphere of normal life than is pos-
sible for their parents.

It is estimated that six million Belgian francs are spent
annually in such aid to D.P.s. The value of it in non-material
terms cannot be put in figures, it is incalculable.

It works like a kind of 'celestial mechanics', the D.P. and
his sponsor making mutual use of the lever or fulcrum.
Many people are sceptical of the whole idea of sponsorship,
but that is because they have never known loneliness and
the complete loss of their place in society. In fact, the
arrival of a letter may revive living springs in the hearts
of refugees which even they believed had dried up. Here are
some examples:

It is nine years now since I had word of my parents . . . You
would not understand the good a correspondence with you can
do me, in giving me back some confidence in life. It is almost as
if it came from home.

Wladimir Jasczenke

For us, who are already old and have spent twenty-nine years
vegetating far from our own country, every kind word is good
for our morale. It would be a great pleasure to correspond with
you.

Mr. Boudny

All the nice chit-chat in your letter made me tremendously
happy. It takes me back into the past, and I have the illusion
that I am not altogether 'without roots'. The thought gives me
strength, and I feel that, in spite of my illness, I could move
mountains. You do not know how terrible it is to feel alone in
the world, and how good and pleasant to have someone who
thinks of you from time to time.

Nikolaus Petruschak

I was astonished to get your letter, and thank you heartily for it : so, all the world has not quite forgotten us! My friends and I have for so long felt they had.

Bogomir Milojevic

How did you know of my existence? I am happy and delighted to have received, for the first time in all these long years of exile, a letter so kindly, so full of sympathy and friendly goodwill. I, who had thought of myself as so forsaken, so useless!

I need your sympathy so much, and your letter has given me new strength and courage, so that I shall more easily bear my loneliness and the wretchedness of my position.

Your letter has done me almost as much good as if I had received it from my mother, whom I have not seen in six years. When I was well, I did not feel so wretched and sad at being far from home, but in the last two years, I have had to wander like a vagrant in foreign countries, which has seriously affected my health although I am still only twenty-six. This terrible illness would not be so hard to bear if one could be looked after by one's own people.

Dear Madame, you are the first person in six years to take an interest in me. No one has asked me whether I was hungry, if I had any money, or if I knew of somewhere to sleep . . .

Your charming letters and the books you send do me so much good they are like fresh air in a sickroom! What you write is full of youthful idealism, difficult to put into practice here under the primitive conditions in which we live, but without it all life of the intellect ceases. For this fine youthfulness of soul which gives fresh life to mine, that felt grown old with suffering, I thank you with all my heart.

I am deeply touched by what you write, for you cannot know what it is to have lost everything. It is long since anyone had a kind word for us, and we have lost faith in mankind. Hitherto we have known nothing but distress, poverty and want, and now I have just received a letter from an absolute stranger in a foreign country, a friendly letter which is not a mere matter of empty words but evidence of a kind heart ready to help.

This letter is the most precious gift you could send. Your compassionate kindness consoles us greatly.

This is how the 'godchildren' wrote, but what of their 'godfathers' and 'godmothers', who were they? They appeared from nowhere after having heard Father Pire on the radio, or after reading an article on D.P.s, or just because the word got round. Requests like these came into the office of the Aid for Displaced Persons.

It is less than five minutes since your broadcast on 'Family Mutual Aid' came to an end, and I was overwhelmed by your stories of these unhappy people, homeless, exiled, and with no means of support. We must indeed come to the aid of the Hard Core and I should like, as far as my means allow, to help one of these poor lonely souls. I am very young—seventeen—and a dressmaker by trade, but I should like to make life easier for one of those poor old people. Having lost a grandfather whom I adored, I should like to be 'godmother' to an old gentleman . . .

Following the Radio-Luxembourg appeals for the unfortunate people still detained in the camps, we should like to become sponsors. We are a young couple, with only a wage to supply our needs and build our little nest, or we should like to do much more, you can be sure, but alas! Still, what we can do, we shall do with all our hearts.

If there be one more destitute, more unfortunate than the rest, be kind enough to put us in touch with him.

In the hope that our modest gesture will bring a little happiness to a soul in distress . . .

I have heard your radio appeal for Displaced Persons. Alas, I am not well-to-do, and so it is only as a correspondent that I come forward. I have myself had a far from easy life, and have had to work to bring up my two children, so that I know what it is to be a 'woman on her own' and understand the mental anguish of these people . . . I enclose a twenty franc note to buy some tobacco or other little comfort for some unhappy soul.

Having heard your appeal for Displaced Persons, I should be

very happy to take part, though very modestly, in the campaign you are launching for the sponsorship of old people in the camps.

Since I am a woman of the working class, my monetary resources are not large, but I should take the greatest pleasure in sending a few little comforts to one of your protégés, and to correspond with him, while trying not to weary him too much . . .

I have heard your radio appeal. I am a girl of working-class family and I am willing to correspond with one of your protégés. I can promise no more because we are not wealthy, but with the pocket money my parents give me, I will try to spoil him . . .

Hearing your appeal for these poor, abandoned people, I thought it best to send you our address, limited though our means are, so that even so we may try to help you in helping them. It is very painful to hear such sad tidings of these people who have as much right to happiness here on earth as we ourselves, and may well be more deserving. Old people should end their days happily after a life of toil, and we young ones can still have our pleasant memories, be it only that of having given a little happiness to a heart nearly worn out. We have a little girl of eight who is waiting impatiently for your instructions as to what we should do, for she wants to share with us in your great work.

And the little girl of these kindly people writes:

I should like it very much if you would answer Mummy because I could do beautiful drawings for these poor, unhappy people.

A little girl who so much wishes that all the world loved one another.

                                                                    Liliane

It is not enough to know how people first came to offer themselves as sponsors, or the reaction prompted by the arrival of their first letters. We must follow up in detail

*some attempts at rescue, whether they turned out to be
successful, frustrated, or even catastrophic.*

*Father Pire's files are full of lengthy reports, written in
the awkward style of translations, but their rather dry
exactness gives at least a faithful picture of the sad world
of the D.P.s. Let us begin with a story that is only partly one
of success:*

The sponsors are French : a schoolteacher's family living in
the department of Haute-Vienne. They were entrusted with the
sponsorship of a Czech refugee family, the family R., then in
Passau, Germany.

R. himself was born on the 17th September 1918, and served
in the Czech army. He helped many of his compatriots to escape
and then got away himself, arriving in Germany in 1951. During that year he was under care for six weeks at Erlangen, and
was afterwards first at Valka then Passau. He gives no detailed
account of his past, but one thing is certain : he is very ill indeed. His wife suffers apoplectic attacks and her health generally is precarious. They are extremely poor, living on public
assistance, and though their quarters are clean, the furnishings
are miserable; they lack everything.

The sponsorship was begun on 13th July 1954. The first report of the social worker on the spot reads : 'The family is
rather a difficult one, and I was at some pains to discover
whether the money and parcels had been received. Madame R.
asserted that she had received nothing, but inquiry at the Post
Office revealed that what had been sent had certainly reached
the family.'

A second report, two months later : 'R. is in prison for having
sold a motor-cycle he had borrowed. The family has a very bad
reputation.' The social worker goes on to express the opinion
that it would be better to help a family more worthy of interest.

The Displaced Persons Organization explained to the French
sponsor that it was up to him whether he ceased or continued
his sponsorship, and he wrote back to us :

'You sent me news of Monsieur R.'s imprisonment following
his theft of a motor-cycle and of the family's bad reputation.

'Allow me to thank you most sincerely for telling me this.
Without wishing to take these unfortunate people to task for

their conduct—how far is it the responsibility of us all, rather than theirs alone?—it is yet helpful to us to know how our godchildren behave. It is equally reassuring that you are always there, and have not launched us on an adventure without being ready to stand by us.

'Since your letter, my wife and I have sent the R. family a money order. It was Madame R. who acknowledged it, telling us that her husband had gone off after selling everything the household possessed, even to beds and clothing.

'Is Monsieur R. still in prison, or was it after his release that he left his wife? How much reliance can we place on what Madame R. tells us? Our decision will depend on whatever information you may kindly give us. If Madame R. can keep a home together for her children—she is expecting another—why should she not be helped to do so?

'Anyway, we will go on writing to Madame R. for a while longer: we should very much like to alleviate a little of this distress, which is something we have never ourselves experienced.'

On receiving this letter we at once replied, saying how heartened we were by their understanding attitude towards the D.P.s and by their anxiety to help them. We decided to undertake a closer examination of the exact situation of their godchildren. In August 1955 another social worker's report was sent on to the sponsors: 'Things are very difficult in the R. family. On the one hand, I should like to help Madame R., but on the other, I would not wish the gifts sent by the sponsors to be destroyed by Monsieur R. in one of his fits of rage, or the money to be diverted to his own purposes. There are two children in the family, and Madame R. is expecting a third. Relations between the husband and wife are very bad. Monsieur R. suffered a head wound in the war and is sometimes seized with a senseless rage to destroy. The couple have already come to blows from time to time, and it was after one of these battles that the wife left their home with the children and attempted to reach Belgium. She was arrested at Aix-la-Chapelle by the German police for illegally crossing the frontier, and was sent back to Passau, but her husband had in the meantime completely cleared the house and sold everything, even the furniture. He disappeared altogether for a fortnight, but eventually applied to the social assistance people for money to make the return trip to Passau. The couple have since been re-united.

The sponsorship continued, but in June 1958 the godfather wrote to us that he was worried by the silence of his godchildren. 'The last letter from Monsieur R. was dated 6th February 1958 and gave bad news of Madame R.'s difficult confinement and of their money worries.' After that, in spite of money having been twice remitted, the sponsor had no further word and asked us for news of the health of the parents and children. On our receipt of this letter an enquiry was made on the spot. In Octoebr we were sent the following report : 'Madame R. is very often ill and can only do the bare minimum of housework. The children unfortunately look very uncared for. The best way to help them all would be to send a little money so that the social worker on the case could take the family's measurements, especially those of the children, and buy what clothes they most need.

The sponsors have since continued to help the family R., using the social worker as their agent. They persevere, waiting, they say, until they can lend a hand with the children's schooling.

After this partial failure, let us look at a resounding success. A Brussels engineer, with his wife and small daughter, found themselves entrusted with the sponsorship of a family of stateless persons, refugees in Austria. The wife, Antonia K., was thirty-three years old and had had a grammar-school education. Her husband, six years older, was a civil servant. Their three children were aged nine, four, and three years.

The sponsorship began in the January of 1956, and in the same month of the next year the godmother's sister wrote to us : 'My sister's sponsorship is one of the successful kind. She is highly intelligent, generous, well-to-do, and a wonderful organizer—all the gifts one could wish for in someone trying to put these unfortunate people on their feet again. They had been going downhill fast, I believe, at the time when she first intervened. The mother had just left hospital in a very run-down condition with a ten-day-old baby in her arms, and the family had no money, no shoes to their feet, no fuel for heating, no layette for the child—in short, they were in such a state that there was no way out of their misery but collective suicide.

'My sister began by enclosing a cheque with her first letter, even at the risk of giving offence to these people she had never met. It was used to buy coal. Before this, the little stove which was all they had in the two rooms, one above the other, which they occupied, had never been lit for three years! The mother —a good intelligent woman, with a knowledge of four languages—from that moment, and without quite realizing where this godsend had come from, most movingly vowed her gratitude to my sister and placed full confidence in her. She wrote that, without her, she would surely have lost at least one of her children, for many D.P.s had died of cold during the hard spell of last February. Many more parcels were sent as soon as possible, and my sister still sends a big one and a cheque each month. The little girl had a little outfit for her first communion, her mother had been able to give some attention to her own appearance, and so on. But, and this seems to me most valuable for their future, one gift of money was used to buy a bicycle for the father which so cut down his travelling time to and from work that he was able to allow himself from two to three extra hours of sleep every day. His spirits improved and, the *curé* of the group having paid his fees for a course of evening classes, he resumed his studies (in accountancy, I believe) in the hope of one day increasing his earning power. So, there you are Father Pire, here is one household in which hope has been reborn and where the children, who are much amused at the idea of "Father going back to school", have learnt to laugh again. Isn't that splendid, Father, and exactly what you wanted?'

In the following weeks, the godmother and her sister recommended this family again and again for the European Village of Bregenz. The family was accepted in May 1957 and settled in. The godmother continued to correspond with them and send regular aid, and when Father Pire was able to pay them a visit in 1958 he wrote to her: 'I spend several hours with your godchildren, and if you can ever come yourself it will be a red-letter day for them.

'As far as day-to-day living is concerned they are not so well placed as you may believe. They had to have a loan to buy furniture, and though all is well on this score, the husband earns a very poor salary. His morale is low and he suffers from a stomach ulcer. Still, we shall be keeping a constant and affectionate eye on them, and I have already written to the husband to tell him how I feel about his return to normal life. Be assured that I am full of hope, for they are very intelligent people, and they have very fine, well-behaved children. But, just the same, they are existing at the moment on a very meagre income, something like three thousand Belgian francs a week, and there are six of them! They have a morbid fear of catching some illness, and not being able to go out any more—that is why they put the last money you sent them away in the bank. I believe there is nothing more I can usefully say about that, but I am very afraid that they are not feeding themselves properly. Madame K. is extremely thin, and I advised her to see a doctor. I am looking for a second sponsor who can give some indirect aid by paying their rent, so that they shall not have the feeling of being so directly dependent on others, and in this way we may gently compel them to devote the money you send to buying food. I will keep you informed and thank you with all my heart for what you have done.'

The godmother continues to send the family the aid necessary until they shall be able to depend solely on their own efforts.

The sponsorship archives are full of such stories of salvaged lives, and among them one can find cases which are as touching as they are quaint. Someone in Antwerp became godmother to Madame S. F., a Russian lady over seventy years of age, and a refugee in Germany since 1944.

Formerly, Madame S. F. was a reporter in Russia—a specialist, a racing journalist! Even now she writes without stopping, no doubt at work on her memoirs. She cannot bring herself to enter a home for, she says, peace and quiet are essential to a writer. Madame S. F. lives in an attic in a Munich suburb, frail in health and under-nourished. This is what her godmother wrote after a visit to her godchild:

During our holidays this year my husband and I visted Germany and Austria, and went to see Madame F. She lives in

Munich, though not in the camp there. She is a charming, and really remarkable old lady. She was formerly a well-known writer on the Turf at Warsaw racecourse, where she earned her living between the wars. Her chief pleasure and interest in life is her very frequent visits to the Munich course, where she is allowed in anywhere, from the cheapest to the most expensive stands. The lady therefore insists that she must be near the racecourse, but the tiny room she has in a small house in the suburbs, is really terrible minute, very much of an attic, and only dimly lit by a little window barely more than a foot square. Moreover, it is badly ventilated and, since it is literally up in the roof, either very hot or very cold. Madame F. suffers badly from asthma, especially in winter, when she stays in bed pretty well all the time. The room is unhealthy for her, and I write to you because I know you have a German social worker in Munich, and I wonder whether it might not be possible to find another rather larger room and, above all, better lit and ventilated. My husband was truly appalled by what he saw. But, Madame F. would never consent unless her new home was somewhere near the thoroughbreds!

Here is the case of A. R., a forty-nine-year-old Yugoslav, formerly a barrister: he was stranded in Germany in 1940, having fled from Italy where both he and his brother had been arrested. His brother had been condemned to twenty-six years' imprisonment, but he himself managed to escape, though only to be incarcerated in Sachsenhausen concentration camp. He never left it until liberated by the Americans in 1945, but by then he was broken in body, blind in one eye, and lame, having been used as a guinea-pig in medical experiments. As he was very feeble, no social assistance was forthcoming for him. Father Pire found him a French godmother who sent him money to buy a box of paints, which he wanted primarily to take his mind off his troubles, but also to make an attempt at earning a little money from the sale of the pictures he would produce. Some while later the social worker, acting for the godmother, sent in the following report:

Three weeks ago, Mr. R., who was formerly at Berlin, was admitted to a home in Bavaria, where he is undergoing treatment for alcoholism, and where he will be taught a trade as soon as he is well enough.

The godmother must not be alarmed when she hears of the six-month cure to which we are submitting him. Mr. R., poor soul, has never got over the bad times he suffered during the war. He has continually lost ground in his disgust with a life which seemed to have nothing worth while to offer, and he took to drink in despair. When we offered him the chance of treatment and of becoming a self-respecting man again, he had the strength of will to rise to the occasion, and since he has been at the home we have had enthusiastic letters from him. He is in love with the place, which is magnificently run, the patients being very well cared for, and we persuaded him to try and trace his relatives in Yugoslavia. In this he has succeeded, for he tells us in his most recent letter that he has had an answer from his sister, the first family contact he has made in fifteen years. His family, all except his mother, who was convinced he was alive and went on praying for him, had believed him dead. It is very important that Mr. R. should see that new hope has dawned, and that he should be surrounded by the friendliness essential to his cure. We hope with all our hearts that his sponsorship will be a success.

Here is the case of Ivan R., a forty-two-year-old blind Ukrainian, formerly a schoolteacher. Arriving in Austria in 1944, he was a chauffeur until 1946, when he lost his sight following an accident.

His wife left him, taking with her their two children, and managed to emigrate to America: he has since had no word, either of her or the children. With no resources of his own, he now lives on Public Assistance. The Aid for Displaced Persons organization gave him as godmother a shorthand-typist in Brussels, who had been a captain of a blind Girl-Guide troop, and she tried to help her protégé, not merely with money, but by sending him a textbook to help him learn Braille. A family at St. Martin's camp set themselves to help him to learn to read and write, and his godmother herself went to see him.

'Last August,' she says, 'I was in Villach and found my godson in good health. I taught him the Braille alphabet, and he knew all his letters in three days. He is full of courage, in spite of his sad plight. You may always count on me to help him or any other D.P. in any way I can. I have seen how hard their lives may be—their unhappiness, their uncertainty about the future, and, above all, their loneliness. To see a D.P. camp, is to feel a sense of responsibility towards these people. We, who have everything, ought at least to give them a little of ourselves!'

You want to hear about a really cheerful case? Here it is. After hearing a lecture by Father Pire, someone in Brussels asked for a sponsorship and was put in touch with C. S., an old White-Russian emigré who had lived in Yugoslavia from 1920 to 1944, and had then had to flee to Austria, where he found shelter in a camp. He is the sole survivor of a family of twenty, his wife and children having stayed in Russia. After some months of correspondence, the godmother went to visit C.

'It was a surprise visit,' she says. 'He was sitting under a tree near another white-haired old gentleman with the fearsome teeth of a retired general. We had been admiring his turn-out and appearance—hat, overcoat and suit, a handsome cane which he wielded elegantly, lively and very expressive little eyes, and an amusingly neatly trimmed moustache—in short, he was extremely prepossessing. Someone called over to him and he stopped his game of cards on catching sight of us, and took us into his quarters while someone went to fetch his devoted lady interpreter. She kindly told us all about his health, his worries, and so forth.

'His room was fairly large, the doorway decorated with flowering branches and the floor strewn with leaves and blossom in honour of Whitsuntide. A single flower ornamented the table, and he insisted on our taking it home with us to Belgium. Although we had just dined, he obliged us to have something to eat and made some tea. He was sorry to have had no warning of our arrival, but it was better so, or he would have run into some extravagance.

'As we walked along arm-in-arm, he called out to everyone: "This is my godmother!" It was really touching, he was such a dear old gentleman.

'When he took us into his room we had been very moved to see that the photographs I had sent him had all been carefully framed, and my husband, something of a sceptic, has been completely won over and now takes an interest in D.P.s himself.'

But sometimes sponsorships have a heart-breaking ending. In spite of proffered friendship and lavish help, it can happen that a D.P. is too broken by his sufferings, that the uprooted tree has had to wait too long for the new rich soil and cannot make new growth.

A woman at Liège had interested herself in an invalid Ukrainian, fifty-one years old and a veteran of both wars. During the second he lost both feet when a shell exploded, and had since lived miserably enough in an Austrian camp, but the sponsorship seemed to be developing in the usual way, and the godmother was able to feel that she had put fresh heart into the poor cripple. Then, one day, she received a letter:

Please send me nothing more, for I am already as good as dead. I return your photo, and thank you for all your kindness. May you have a happy Christmas. Twice already, I have written to say that I should not live much longer, and now I write my last letter. You have been kind to me, dear Mother, but I shall die on the eighteenth of the month. I wish you every good fortune, Mother dear.

It is as if you were both my mother and my dear wife . . .

This D.P. committed suicide.

CHAPTER ELEVEN

Money

YOU SIT THERE *facing me still, Father, but I no longer seem to recognize you. The story of your life had been running like a clear stream, and now it suddenly disappears below ground. As far as conventional biography goes, Father Pire does not seem to exist, why is that?*

You are right there, answered Father Pire. Until I came in contact with the refugees, I had a body, soul and strong will of my own. After that, I felt myself dissolving, lost in their distress: the little stream had rushed into the great muddy river. As I have told you: I cannot reintegrate myself except through prayer.

You have been alive, though, all these ten years?

I am not so sure! Obviously, I have gone through the motions of living, have been physically present as I carried out my work, but even as I organized it, wrote my letters, spoke in public, travelled here and there, another man suffered somewhere inside me at every moment—the worthwhile suffering born of compassion. Every morning Humanity in Distress has joined me at table. The Refugee never allows himself to be forgotten: if I am eating, I think of what he eats, and if you hand me a glass of water, it sometimes seems like a glass of tears.

138

Yet, Father Pire has been alive, very much so ...

On his return from the Austrian camps in May 1949, he began to tie up the threads of the sponsorships. But, at the same time, he was still curé of La Sarte, and busied himself with his parish, his work for poor children. He thought of tomorrow, not yet of the day after. Meanwhile, his work became overwhelming, and he had to have a secretary. One of the Open-air Mission counsellors, Mademoiselle Jolling, had studied sociology and Father Pire asked for her help. Not for long, of course, perhaps a fortnight, just to put the mail in order. In 1960, Mademoiselle Jolling is still putting the mail in order, more than ten years later. From time to time, as a matter of principle, she tenders her resignation.

The 'central office' of the Aid for Displaced Persons had at first been set up in the rectory, where a wooden partition divided the parlour in two. Then Father Pire had an office in the town, in the Rue du Marché. A programme of action, an office and mail: it needed only this for trouble to start.

In Belgium the fraternal world of charity is sharply divided, for example, between right-wing and left-wing organizations. It is also somewhat bureaucratic and smaller enterprises tend to be absorbed. In particular, there is the Catholic central organization, very proud of having the sanction of the bishops, and while showing itself worthy of their mandate, sometimes thinking of it as a concession of a monopoly. This centripetal charity controls all Catholic good works, not excepting their finances.

Accustomed to power, it has become a trifle autocratic. And, moreover, its charity is dispensed according to denominational principles. Now Father Pire had from the start disregarded such limitations: confronted with some poor soul, he saw only that he was in want, and heeded neither his faith nor his lack of one. But he was a priest, and they wanted his work in their official records! He flatly refused and a certain coolness resulted.

Father Pire has never said a word about such difficulties. But, when he was awarded the Nobel Peace Prize the joy of some, the resentment of others, as well as inevitable human curiosity, led to a certain report being dug out again from various ecclesiastical drawers. Sent to all Belgian bishops ten years previously by the central organization I have just been talking about, it evinced a pained surprise on account of this bold Dominican. What was this? Someone unwilling to submit to rules and controls, someone who ignored even percentages? It was unforgivable.

I reproduce only one argument put forward in this masterpiece. The gist of it is: 'By his refusal to have his work entered on our records, Father Pire weakens Catholic statistics, and may so put them in an inferior position as compared with Protestant statistics.'

Always this apostolate on the attack, this competitive charity . . .

The work of sponsorship had enjoyed great success in France from the very beginning, and here the same 'protectionist' reactions manifested themselves. A French bishop addressed a circular letter to all Belgian bishops, of which the general sense was as follows:

Father Pire's work is extravagant in the full meaning of the word. Moreover it is a Belgian project, so what is it doing in France? Finally, it is a neutral work . . .

Neutral!

Such murmurings went far. In Belgium, the farthest they could go was to Malines, seat of the Archbishopric and of the Belgian Catholic authority. Malines heard them thought the matter over, and kept silent. Henceforth, Father Pire might not have existed. His work was not hampered, it was just ignored. At the time of the Nobel award, when congratulations arrived from the whole world, only

*one telegram was missing from the touching series of mes-
sages: the one from Malines. But, maybe it went astray . . .*

*To make an end of such items, one can just note that left-
wing charitable organizations were no more favourable in
their attitude. After the award of the Nobel Prize to Father
Pire, a rash of ill-tempered pamphlets appeared, which
were not at all tender of the prize-winner's feelings. A
joint communiqué was issued by several big charitable
associations, both lay and secular, sealed in a temporary
alliance by their extraordinary grudge. 'Allowing the
figures to speak for themselves', it was intended to show
that Father Pire's work had never been other than infinitesimal. As far as numbers go, this is true enough, but his
opponents either forget or pass over in silence the quality
of its devotion. The Nobel Foundation showed sound judgement in rewarding the unremitting, disinterested effort of
a man working alone, without funds, without influence,
but inspired by a sense of human brotherhood.*

*They weighed in the balance, monied bureaucracy on
the one hand, against radiant human warmth on the other,
and watched the scale go down on the side of a loving-
kindness that weighed heavier than the whole shining universe.*

*When I talked with him about those great refugee 'fac-
tories' where emigrants are selected from the mass by
purely utilitarian circles, Father Pire expressed neither ap-
proval nor disapproval. He did not comment on the aims
of others, merely tried to define his own:*

I have never wanted my work to turn into a system, he
said. Even in establishing a certain minimum organization
and degree of method, my work quickly expanded beyond
my personal ability to cope with it, and I had to choose
some assistants, but I took great pains to maintain the per-

sonal character of our work, in spite of this expansion. I think I have managed it. I have remained at the craftsman level, the craftsman working with the aid of his family, and have not founded a factory. Some have reproached me for that. I know that some people said, after the award of the Nobel Prize to me: 'We should have had it, we would have achieved ten times more!'

They deserved it, Father, if weight of numbers is all . . .
He made no reply, but went on with his argument.

The answer to these problems of the charitable fraternity is to work simply and harmoniously as a team.

I have tried to ensure that the people working for me should work as if for themselves, and this they have succeeded in doing. Each morning we plunge back into the world's misery with a compassion that seems as if newly reborn each night. One might say that those who work with me have been sent by Providence, for I have followed no set method in finding them.

Perhaps it is because your fellow-workers have not joined
your team for the sake of money?

Perhaps. My employees are not highly paid and could earn more elsewhere, yet they stay with me. Why? I cannot explain it, except that they have some special quality of heart and soul. Obviously, money is a necessity, but it becomes a pernicious influence when it makes the work of charity a job like any other! As far as I am concerned there are no cushy berths, though that does not mean that I do not pay my workers adequately. Oh no, I consider that all toil is worthy of a wage, but on the other hand it does mean that when it comes to money given for refugees I become something of a miser, even avaricious! I want to devote to them as much as I possibly can.

That is why my general expenses have never risen above twenty per cent, though the big organizations specializing in refugees for export have expenses that are fifty, sixty, or even sometimes seventy per cent of the sums donated for charitable relief. I know of one case in which, out of a gift of a thousand dollars, seven hundred went in general expenses and three to the D.P.s. I must therefore wage a continual war on the financial front, but one concerned far more with putting the money to the most effective and economic use, than with the actual collecting of it.

Where does this money come from?

I have no subsidy, no source of regular income, but I am the father of a very numerous family, and like every other father I work to provide a livelihood for my children. Eight months of the year I devote to the search for funds, which often come from the poor. I have never begged, yet how many times have I received all kinds of little gifts? One day it was a young girl who gave me the gold bracelet she had had for her first communion. Another time, a poor Hungarian servant girl who came up to me and slipped 20 francs into my hand for the refugees. No, I do not beg, I just go everywhere explaining what I do and for whom I do it. Those who understand are fired with a desire to help . . .

And those who do not understand.

I do not want their money. I am not just taking up a collection, I am launching a crusade, and no easy one, I can tell you! A lady, writing to me once about my European Villages, said: 'Isn't it splendid! The European Villages are popping up all over the place, like mushrooms.' Far from it, alas, they don't in the least grow like mushrooms: we have

to win them from the soil with golden trowels and spades.
I receive many small gifts, and, always, I express my gratitude to those who send them. Of the twelve to thirteen
million francs needed to support my Villages and Homes
each year, two-thirds are made up of such small donations.
Once I was given a million Belgian francs, and once five
hundred thousand, from an unknown well-wisher . . . But,
these exceptions apart, even sums of one hundred thousand or two hundred thousand francs are rare. I can assure
you it is the little gifts that matter! You want an example.
Here is the letter a poor old Frenchwoman sent me at
Christmas in 1955:

> I have just sent you a money order for 20,000 francs.
> I have by me some savings, put aside for my old age, and now
> my old age has come. But the thought of you, who have so
> many, many lives plunged into the deepest distress in your care,
> has much troubled me and made me very unhappy.
> The good God has told me what I ought to do, and I send you
> this amount in his name. I hope to repeat the gift twice more,
> that is, until my savings are exhausted.

What could be more greater-hearted or more nobly
simple than that?

The rich have plenty of opportunity to make lordly gestures while still living in luxury. The poor and the sick
should also have their chance to give happiness to others,
and you have seen with what spontaneous generosity and
delicacy of feeling they do it.

But I have never used ignoble means of raising money,
such as linking myself with one particular party, denom-
ination or nation. I could once have received several millions in aid from a certain Government, just by accepting
certain controls and instructions. I refused.

And yet, what can be done without money? At the

present time it takes 60,000 Belgian francs to salvage a D.P. At a single banquet two or three refugees are often eaten! How many, for example, were swallowed up during the Brussels Exhibition! It makes one sick to think of it.

I must also consider the best way of using this money of mine, and I have to be realistic. I received 12 million francs in 1958, and if I had divided it among all the 200,000 refugees, each would have had only 60 francs. It is better to concentrate a thousand times that amount in achieving the complete rescue of one refugee. My twelve million, divided into amounts of 60,000, would only allow me to save two hundred people. After I have passed by the 160,000 people who compose the Hard Core will have been reduced to 159,800 . . . The only regret I have in life is not having more money to devote to the D.P.s. But I must spend what I have intelligently. For example, I bitterly reproach myself for having built poor quality houses in some of my European Villages. One mustn't be the sort of benefactor who builds too well for temporary purposes and too badly for anything permanent.

You have sometimes been deceived, then?

Yes. People have robbed me, betrayed my confidence. It's partly my own fault, for I am easily carried away and have a too trusting disposition. But, if I had not been made that way, should I have done what I have? Basically, my principles are more fit for Paradise, since I am all for implicit trust, given on the spot, right from the start. If anyone asks me for explanations I am hurt at his lack of confidence in me. Because I put my faith in others so freely, I am astounded when my confidence is not reciprocated. I won't be asked for explanations, especially in financial matters, but I will gladly volunteer information. I have put this department of my work on a legal footing by establishing seven official associations, six national and one international, with registered statutes and boards of directors. Each has an accounts department, under the scrupulous supervision of expert auditors, who check the balance sheets in detail, including the bundles of chits for expenses. My books are open to anyone who cares to inspect them, for I prefer to carry on my work in a glasshouse. It is only by living out in the broad light of day these past ten years, and concealing nothing, either as to finances or ideas, that I have managed to survive. I have fought to ensure that individual liberty of conscience should be respected, and that no one should have a monopoly of charitable works.

That was daring of you, Father.

One of my superiors once characterized me, remember, as 'the acme of timid audacity'. That's how I see myself, and that's how I act.

And is it an instinctive need with you to have everything out in the open?

I think I got this obsession with exactness in my accounts from my father, and also from reading items in the newspapers. People who cook the books are everywhere, even in the religious world, and I have a horror of these tales of clergy who fiddle halfpennies, play the stock market to increase the funds intended for a chapel, and cheat over butter or trade on the Black Market to get money to build a church. All that sort of thing is a trap laid by the Devil. As if a holy purpose could justify lapsing into dishonesty and trickery! Bah!

That is not for me. Besides, didn't Christ say, 'No one can serve two masters: God and Mammon.' And Mammon is money. I never let myself forget that, and people can say of my work anything they please, except that I am a trader out for profit.

In short, for people who work in the Displaced Persons Organization, every day has the same innocence as the first dawn of the world after the creation?

Every day must be filled with living friendship. Friendship is a passion with me, and I need the support it offers; I am no hermit in that respect. I need my daily ration of courage, my fuel, as it were! I look for it from those who work with me and from my mail. My letters are an ever-renewed spiritual mystery, and you can't imagine what emerges from them: joy, sympathy, encouragement and appeals for help. I look for my mail each day as impatiently as a child, and then, in replying, I give to some what I have received from others—filling one with the overflow of another.

Does that mean that everyone in your offices is all smiles and serenity?

Alas, no! I am exacting, perhaps too much so, and I am a demon for method and punctuality. Sometimes this leads to outbreaks of temper. For example, if someone sends off a letter I've dictated and forgets to make me sign it first, then Mr. Pire is far from easy going: he scolds, scowls and is unreasonableness personified. At each confession, I have sins like these to unburden myself of, and I have a long way to go yet in my progress to perfection. I believe that every time God grants us another year of life, it is because we have still something in us on which we can improve. St. Teresa of the Child Jesus, whose picture I keep by my pillow, said: 'Formerly, when I lived in the world, and woke in the morning knowing there were unpleasant things to be faced, I would get up feeling very miserable. Now it is just the opposite, I wake up with the better spirits the more opportunities I foresee to suffer and gain eternal life for my children, for I am a mother of souls.'

That is the degree of perfection at which I aim.

CHAPTER TWELVE

———————◆———————

Homes for Old People

HE TOOK *a photograph and a letter out of a drawer and held them out to me. The photograph had been taken ten years before in a camp near Linz in Austria, at the time when he made that first momentous visit which changed his life, and it shows him between two old people, husband and wife.*

They were adrift, he said, and life hung as loosely about them as their clothes. Something made me take a note of their names, and that same 'something' impelled me to go beyond the kind of sponsorship which could only alleviate, not entirely dispel, the misery of the D.P.s. From that moment, I was set on getting them right out of the camps.

A year later, that old couple had arrived at my Home at Huy—the first home for aged D.P.s in the world.

No one before you had thought of the idea?

I believe plenty of people had thought of it, but the idea had never been put into practice. I have already spoken of the inhumanity of Governments: the impersonality of administrative routine leads to harshness. Refugees were to be admitted to their countries only on skilled, expert appraisal. Oh yes, gloves were worn during the operation! But, just

149

the same, it was a skimming of the cream, a slave market, a white slave traffic. No one ever came to seek out the refugee in his hut SOLELY for his own good !

The Nations have had the hypocritical, double-faced attitude of the Pharisees, saying to the able-bodied D.P. :

'Enter, my friend, you have good, strong muscles.'
But then they have slammed their doors in the face of the aged and infirm and the handicapped, saying :

'Can't possibly take you in. We have too many foreigners already.' And so they make the pretence of claiming : 'Our consciences are clear, we have done our duty,' even though they have only picked out the 'human assets'. Everywhere it is the same story : 'Come to me, but only if you are going to hew coal . . .'

There is always room, no matter which country is concerned, if it is someone willing and able to do the jobs no one else wants.

If you persist, in spite of everything, in trying to get residence permits for people of the Hard Core, Governments turn a deaf ear, and often reply through their police departments, asking in tones of virtuous indignation : 'Do you want to make my country a refuge for every undesirable ?' If you raise your voice to a shout, a Government will now and again end by granting your request, though still dodging the issue by saying : 'Of course it wasn't we who refused you before, that was just the Police Department.'

It is as if someone kicked you, and then said. 'I am so sorry, that wasn't me, it was my boot who did it ?'

Father Pire paused for breath. He always blazes up when he starts talking about these ruthless entry restrictions the Nations lay down, an egoistic measure which is oddly enough accompanied by an unstinting generosity in offers of money. Hundreds, even thousands of millions of francs have been subscribed by a mere twenty countries to help

*the refugees, but this seeming contradiction is soon resolved
by Father Pire's disillusioned comment:*

'They pay *not* to have them.'

*And what happened, Father, to the two old folk in the
photograph?*

When they came to Huy in 1950 they soon struck root,
and even bloomed again. They lived at the Home, but the
whole town adopted them, and they became a focus of
social activity. Even 'Good Society' received them with
friendliness, but was this because they were old, cleanly,
well mannered, and deserving, or because the husband happened to be a prince? I don't know, and anyway it doesn't
concern me. For three years they were happy—the Prince
was even granted a hunting permit—and then they died
peacefully. In the meantime, others were arriving, not
princes this time, but most of them took root, too. Sometimes, on my way to the office, I would pass my old friend
N. and wish him 'Good morning' as he went down to the
town to make up a game of cards with his friends there. He
had so completely adapted himself that he was beginning
to speak Walloon as well as his native Russian.

*You have told me the story of the photograph, but what
of the letter?*

I made use of the photograph to show what our aim is in
establishing these homes for old people: to rescue a few
refugees completely and genuinely. To give them the
chance of dreaming of their lost countries free from care.
But now let us look at the letter. It came from someone in
the east of Europe and will make you understand why something must be done for them:

Reverend Father,

Having listened to a foreign radio programme on your charitable work, I have summoned up courage to write to you. Now seventy-four years old and blind, I was once a mining engineer. My wife and I are living in one of the East European countries; she is sixty-seven and we have been married fifty years.

Long ago I qualified at the Metallurgical Institute and at once succeeded in obtaining a post as technician at the railway wagon works at X, where I rose in twenty years of service to Chief Engineer. As I had taken out three different patents, I left the factory and established in my native town my country's first enterprise for manufacturing hardened steel. In this way I accumulated a substantial fortune, but my business was nationalized in 19—, without a penny of compensation, and I was also deprived at the same time of the properties I owned, the flat I lived in and my money. From my factory I salvaged only my hat, and I had no time to do more than throw out a few clothes by way of the window when I was evicted from my flat. From that moment, ten whole years ago, I was declared a 'class enemy', and became a Stateless Person inside the borders of my own country. I could get no work, could claim no pension, and was hounded out of my native town. I am leading a wretched life at B., with no rights except to be treated with contempt and subjected to constant humiliation.

Meantime, I have had an eye operation and have only twenty per cent vision, so that I am a member of the Blind Association, though here, too, I qualify for no aid. They would not accept me as a worker in the brush factory run for the blind, even though I offered to work without pay for six months to serve my apprenticeship. Now, I must leave my present flat by May 1st, for in my quality as 'class enemy' I have no right to one. Yet, in all my life, I have never been convicted of any offence.

These years since nationalization have passed in the utmost misery. Most of my generation are already in the cemetery. Everything my wife and I possessed, except the clothes we stand up in, has been sold to buy food, so that we cannot even count on eating tomorrow, quite apart from the fact that we shall be thrown out on the street on the 1st May. It is no use moving to the country because the villages are also 'socialized', and only the very old remain outside the *Kolkhoz*.

But you, Reverend Father, you still live in a free country,

where perhaps some metallurgical engineers or foundry owners might be prepared to extend some small aid to prevent our dying of hunger.

I should be overwhelming grateful if we could be accepted on your recommendation for your home for old people, because I should immediately be granted an exit permit as a 'class enemy.'

At our age, don't let us die in misery.

You need not fear that we have any pretensions left, for in these ten years of unhappiness, we have lost the habit of living well.

I hope and believe that you will hear my very humble prayer.

Here we have two out of the three elements in the problem: the old and their distress. The third is: international precautions.

The export trade in old people is more hedged about with regulations than if they were dynamite. Look a moment at what I had been trying to do since 1953. As *curé* of La Sarte, I still paid my twenty-five parochial visits each week, consuming in the process my apples, hot coffee, and chilled wine; I still had my retreats, my study groups, my confessions, my mail, and a thousand D.P. sponsorships.

Now, on top of all this, I was trying to get old people out of the camps. It was very difficult. First of all, I must get residence permits for them, and I succeeded in obtaining twenty valid for Belgium. But I must then give a written undertaking to the I.R.O. and the Belgian Government that I would take over responsibility for these D.P.s I was bringing in for the rest of their lives. That is to say, I must promise to house them, feed them, clothe them, supply their medical needs ... even provide a coffin.

Even that, Father?

Even that ... Further, I must engage never to apply for aid to the State, the Provincial Government, the Parish Council, the Public Assistance organization, or the Mutual Assurance Societies. At that time it cost me 1,500 Belgian francs a month for each old person to maintain these refugees, but nowadays my budget for the homes has risen to three millions annually. Three millions to be found year in year out with the aid of Providence! In 1950 I had at my disposal some 200,000 francs and a certain amount of moral credit, and this is what I told them at the Genevan headquarters of the I.R.O. But moral credit got me nowhere, what was needed was just plain credit! Eventually though, they let me have twenty old people. I had rented a house, once a baker's shop, next door to my office at Huy. I waited a month, two months, then three, and still the old people had not arrived. The formalities were long drawn out, partly due perhaps to financial precautions. Actually, a lump sum of 400 to 1,000 dollars is paid by the international organizations on the release of a D.P., this grant being meant to cover travelling expenses and the cost of settling them in, but the system led to abuses and mistakes. Certain sharp practitioners went and routed the old people out of the camps, and then took advantage of age-old local regulations to foist them on the homes run by religious houses, while they pocketed the dollar allowance themselves. This meant old-style workhouse accommodation, with dormitories and refectories, in short, communal life. Moreover, it also meant the old couples would be separated, the husbands in the men's section and the wife in the women's. There were even suicides.

The D.P.s were all the more distressed by these archaic institutions, in that most of them had belonged in their native lands to the intellectual classes. Now these workhouses and asylums had originally been intended as a refuge for the working-class poor, who in their old age would find an existence there less harsh than they had known in their working life. For them it represented a step up, but the D.P.s were going down one, and there lay the tragedy.

You cannot imagine how dilapidated those places were, how out-dated their regulations. One day, I had occasion to interest myself in an old man whom some good Belgian nuns had taken in to the almshouse attached to their convent. The poor old fellow was pining away for lack of some corner in which he could have some privacy and be by himself. His sponsor offered to pay for a screen partition to be put up round his bed, and this grave matter was considered by the Mother Superior. She did not dare make the decision : 'I shall have to refer back to our Mother General in Rome,' she told me.

Can you imagine such a thing?

But let us return to my converted baker's shop in Huy. We worked like slaves to get it ready, and then we waited. We waited a long time and we gradually became very anxious. Then, one evening, when I had already gone back to the monastery, some of my workers who were sorting out old clothes had the fantastic notion of dressing themselves up as elderly D.P.s and telephoning my secretary that the first contingent had just arrived by train at Huy station! They knew that would make Tintin come running.

Tintin, who is that?

Oh, that's what we call Mademoiselle Jolling at the Displaced Persons organization, and I believe that even at the Nobel Foundation in Norway she is known by that name, I am happy to say.

Well, Tintin fell into the trap, only too completely! Before rushing out of the office, she telephoned me in a fever of excitement: 'Father, they are here!'

I raced down from the monastery in a tearing hurry, and came on them in full masquerade. Lord, what a disappointment it was! I just burst into tears, and my young ones, seeing this, themselves followed suit. We made a ridiculous picture, but it shows how strung up we were.

At last my old people did arrive. On 2nd September 1950. How moved we were as we watched them alight from the train, and how touching was their happiness.

They settled down very quickly, and, seeing them so calm and collected, one would never guess what they had gone through. One of our old couples, eight-five years old, had been abandoned in the Austrian camp by their two daughters who had found work in America. Another old couple had at one time agreed to go to France, but, although they had been married fifty years, they would have had to live separately. Another long-married pair, after experience of seven camps, had been stranded in a room they had to share with six others. In our Homes each couple found themselves in a large room where they could live in peace in a family atmosphere, their hearth and home at last restored to them, and I respected this happiness absolutely. So, if either husband or wife died, the survivor kept on the same room alone, until ready to join the one who had passed on. Even though I had so long a waiting list and so few places to fill, I would not disturb again the modest home to which so many memories were already linked, nor have the lonely survivor once more uprooted.

Therefore, one of my Homes is occupied almost entirely by widows and widowers. So much the better. We shall wait.

What do these refugees transplanted into one of your Homes say about the change?

Usually this: 'We used to be just D.P.s, but now we are human beings again.'

Father, how did you set about getting the money?

I asked for it! I gave lectures, made radio appeals, campaigned in the press. I gave my first lecture at a Rotary Club before a group of manufacturers. I was sick with fright, because I thought I should have some pretty hard hearts to tackle, but how wrong I was! There is nothing to stop a man being compassionate at the same time as he turns out steel railway lines.

After my second lecture, given before the Rotary Club at Verviers, a wool town, someone sent me twenty-five mattresses, absolutely free! Then came pots and pans, plates and dishes, furniture, linen, and bed-coverings.

They gave me wonderful help, so that we were able to open a second and larger home at Esneux on 16th June 1951. Later I was to open two more, both in Belgium, one at Aertslaer in 1953 and the other at Braine-le-Comte in 1954. This achievement demanded tremendous efforts from us and we had to learn by experience. To begin with, we advertised in the newspapers that we wanted to rent some houses, and received nearly four hundred replies. We sorted out the most likely and were left with forty-four to view. I inspected them all from the basement to the attic, and it was difficult to make the final choice. Generally, it was better to give preference, not to buildings isolated in the country, but to houses in the heart of the towns, where the old people would be better able to merge with the rest of the community. The only exception I made was in the case of the Château d'Esneux, because it had so many individual rooms. We had then to put the houses in good condition, not always an easy task. For example, at Esneux the steam central-heating system was so antiquated that I had to find myself an almost centenarian technician to get it going.

The home at Braine-le-Comte had its wooden floors waxed, Sunday after Sunday and plank by plank, by our whole team at Huy, including Father Pire. If my devoted fellow-workers could give up their week-ends, I could not let them out-distance me, so I waxed too. At other times we sorted the gifts. Some were magnificent, but I also found the most incongruous objects descending on me. Muffs and umbrellas, old moth-eaten couches and mahogany beds, and tattered linen riddled with holes. Sometimes an old radio set: 'If you put in three new valves and a condenser it will go splendidly again,' they said when they made us the offer. And there were old toys galore. In short, we could have stocked a museum, and costumed a whole theatrical company specializing in Victorian drama, we had such a collection of long skirts, whalebone corsets, and hats of our grandmother's day. Some households imagined they were following the example of St. Martin, who gave his cloak to a beggar, if they designed to pass on to us their moth-eaten greatcoats.

These people would have died of shame to see Christ dressed in clothes such as they gave us. Saddest of all were the gifts of underclothing, absolutely in tatters! We would never dare to send such things to our refugees. I can always hear what a wretched D.P., who yet kept his self respect, once said to me:

'It is always painful, Father, to go down in the world, but the greatest humiliation of all is to have to wear second-hand underclothing.'

I am not the only one who understands this. One of my benefactresses, the wife of a patriotic Belgian shot by the Germans, never sends to D.P.s any but new underclothing, and so that they should be the more sure of that, she leaves on the price tickets.

And are all your old people happy? Have they all taken root?

Father Pire's answering smile first broadens and then becomes a gale of laughter. I feel sure I have brought some odd happening back to his mind, and when he explains, I find I am right.

They are happy, and almost all of them are glad to say so. But, since no work is ever perfect, and since I am an absolute brute, I had a couple of Russians specially brought out from the camps so that I could torture them! For ten years they have lived in one of my Homes, and for the whole of that time they have complained of being persecuted. The old lady has even accused me of wanting to strangle her.

Father Pire was helpless with laughter.

They arrived in 1950, he went on, and almost at once an argument started the whole thing off. In all innocence, the lady superintendent of the Home had put this old couple at the same table with two Ukrainians. How strange human beings are! Their distress is never so great that they can't find a way to quarrel over politics, and so we had my two Russians squabbling with the Ukrainians. That sort of thing grows more bitter and its effects spread. One day I happened to be present when one of these brawls was going on, and it made me so angry that I shouted at them. From that moment the old lady proclaimed that I wanted to strangle her. She and her husband decided on the spot to withdraw to their room, and demanded that their meals be brought to them there. Since they were hale and hearty, this mark of honour was denied them, but they were told that they would be allowed to dine upstairs in their room as often as they wished if they fetched their food themselves. First it was 'No', then it was 'Yes', and then finally 'No'. They turned obstinate, stayed in their room, canvassed public support, and ended by calling in two lawyers. So, there they were, my silly old people, complaining about me to the entire world. They wrote to the Cardinal Primate of Belgium, to the Prime Minister, to the Red Cross, to the High Commissioner for Refugees at Geneva, and to the Vatican! One day, when Queen Elisabeth of Belgium paid a visit to the home, they purposely dressed themselves up in their oldest and dirtiest clothes, and managed to say to her, 'Your Majesty, you haven't replied to our letter.' Then they issued a writ against the superintendent of the Home.

They had just remembered that the I.R.O. had paid us a settlement grant of 1,600 dollars for them. But that had been six years earlier, and to make the charge more up to date, they totted up the cost of all the meals they hadn't eaten in the dining room in these intervening years, and demanded both repayment of the dollar grant and compensation for the lost meals.

But what had they been living on, Father, in all those years?

He winked at me.

That is exactly what I shall never ask them! he said. Because I know that they had accomplices, other old Russians who secretly took them all those celebrated meals they are supposed not to have eaten, and then they had meals with their friends in the town as well. They told their woeful story so well that people stuffed them.

In the Home itself, everyone knew all about it, and pitied them for their sulky obstinacy and their naïve behaviour.

But that, too, is part and parcel of the D.P. And if I have told you this tale, it is only, once more, so that nothing should be hidden. Rescuing a human being is a difficult and delicate operation, and the graft of new skin does not always succeed, but we keep on trying. My only regret in the case of my old Russians is to think that they may well continue in their obstinacy as long as they live, and that their pigheadedness may end by upsetting the family life of the Home to some extent.

Actually, people do take sides, some being for Russia, others for the Ukraine, but there is nothing one can do about it. They know perfectly well that I shall never send them back. But, when you come down to it, the story is not all that funny.

And have your benefactors over these last ten years never grown weary?

No. There are always some who keep faith, and new kind hearts are always making an appearance. Sometimes even Governments offer me considerable sums, only making the condition that the gift remain secret. Nothing is more oddly touching than this discreet generosity exercised by the Government Official, the apparently surly benefactor. What hidden treasure, what living springs of brotherly kindness there are ! But I must say that I have a little disappointment now and again.

Such as?
He thought a moment, and then began to laugh again, this time with a glint of mischief.

I once offered the Honorary Presidency of one of my work sections to an aristocratic and wealthy public man, already President of another very large charitable body. He accepted, and gave me twenty francs.

CHAPTER THIRTEEN

———————◆———————

Taking Root Again

THAT MORNING *a note of advice had arrived at the office of the Aid for Displaced Persons Organization: two cheques had been registered to their account, one from Freemason Lodge X, the other from the Bishop of Z.*

After musing a moment on the coincidence that cheques should arrive from two such divergent sources at the same time, he picked up his suitcase, got into his black car, and was off to Spiesen, near Saarbrucken, to lay the foundation stone of the fifth European Village, the Albert Schweitzer.

Once more he travelled along the great German corridor which runs through to Austria and comprised the area which is the nebulous realm of the D.P.s. He was crossing into Germany, that great swirling churn of refugees, where little by little the skimming of the cream from the milk is being completed. He was plunging to its bottom, going once more into the saddening atmosphere of poverty and discouragement.

Rolling along the motorway, he thought of the mail he had just been reading. An asthmatic old lady, a D.P. in Augsburg, was feeling the cold. She would like to be able to have hot infusions and vapours to inhale, but to prepare these she must have an oil stove.

'She needs an oil stove,' thought Father Pire, and said the words over to himself so that they sank into his mind and served to take him back into the world of the D.P.s.

Here we are living in towns which are crammed with oil stoves, some of us so used to turning obedient gas taps or electric switches that we have forgotten what an oil stove looks like, and it takes us some concentrated thinking to realize that in the mind of an asthmatic old lady D.P. an oil stove is an unattainable, heavenly invention.

Among the letters there had also been one from a young Hungarian couple. The man and wife, both D.P.s, had managed to resume their medical studies at Frankfurt, but now there was a baby on the way. Absolute treason in administrative eyes! The wife automatically lost her student grant, and would have to break off her studies because of the baby. Her husband would be compelled to do the same since, without the grant, he would have to work to support both wife and child.

Father Pire gave a sigh. Along the road the countryside was a shambles, scattered with refuse, bits of this and pieces of that. There was an old prisoner-of-war camp here, still in use thirteen years after the end of the war, but now the inhabitants were D.P.s. One could not get away from D.P.s.

These, like so many others, came from Eastern Europe. Everything was cut off to the east by the Iron Curtain, and no refugee ever wanted to return and be merged once more with the millions beyond that frontier. But the West had its curtain, too, a strong invisible, nylon network of regulations and national self interests. The Governments wielding their scoops and skimming ladles stirred the cauldron up and left the residue behind. It is the familiar story of the earlier pages of this book, always it is the Hard Core that remains. The refugee problem is always with us, but no one wants to get down to dealing with it, they just hope it will eventually solve itself.

Father Pire stepped on the accelerator and left the rags, the torn bits of bitumenized cardboard behind. He saw the *pale-faced children bent over the yellowing stumps of a field of cabbage. The dead stalks were like D.P.s—hundreds of thousands of uprooted plants, hastily 'heeled in' again in old barrels and packing-cases, clumsily shoved into pots any old how.*

The metaphor had a literal truth! Would it ever be possible to tranplant them properly again, and where were the flower beds even to try?

But I am the gardener of the Almighty, thought Father Pire, I must carry on with my hoeing and they will flower again, even though they may not be prize blooms.

The difficulties in the way were engraved on his heart . . . He encountered them every day in the Homes for Old People.

'To give back to the old people their lost country.' That was a stumbling block to come a cropper upon. It was one thing to dream of doing it and quite another to bring it to realization. Space and Time had created an enormous gulf which cut them off with no way round, and time was ever deepening and widening it, so that the old people, standing with their arms outstretched to the further shore, saw it ever retreating from them and becoming at last indistinct. Their native lands were farther and farther away, became dim on the horizon, and lost reality. There was nothing to be done about it. Fill every corner of the Homes with icons? Feed their inmates on nothing but borsch and goulash? The salt of their native earth would always be lacking for these old people. In their night sky the stars—Russia, Hungary, Bulgaria, Czechoslovakia, Lithuania, Latvia, Estonia, and the Ukraine—were sinking towards the horizon with the same relentless motion as the constellations.

Because the next day would once more see his wishes realized, Father Pire lingered over his memories. Nine years already gone. Nine years since the words Hard Core had sounded in his heart like an alarm bell. Nine years since he had begun retrieving the 'human surplus'.

Four Homes for Old People; four Villages, and soon there would be another. More than fifteen thousand sponsorships. The burden had been heavy, for to walk along the road of charity is to wear shoes of lead.

He recalled his first year's work, and his joy at establishing the first circuit between the D.P.s and the rest of the world. As with electricity, if the wiring be sound, contact is made and charity passes along it, even if there are a few sparks at first.

One day he had come across a D.P. in camp who was an ex-flying-officer, and had as his godmother a little girl of fourteen. Schoolgirls are supposed to knit comforts, not take up sponsorships, especially when the godchild is a flying-officer.

The cards in the big filing-cabinet devoted to sponsors were soon changed over: the officer was entrusted to a widow and the schoolgirl got a family with three children. Father Pire has great faith in the moral benefits of sponsorship and the subject is often in his thoughts.

Because it is something intangible, lots of people do not believe in it, he reflected, and because you cannot express loving-kindness in statistics, it will never be known in this world just what the sponsorships have meant. The finest things remain hidden.

That evening he arrived at Saarbrucken.

It was a Sunday in September 1958 at Spiesen, in the Saar mining district. It was here that Father Pire wanted to establish his fifth European Village, in that Saar Valley where the Great Powers have tried to bring to birth the spirit of a United Europe, counting on the goodwill of the people of the Saar and perhaps on the war-weariness of Germany and France. It is one of the long-disputed frontier lands. As long ago as the days of Charles V, his Spanish troops and his German mercenaries had crossed over the bridge at Saarbrucken to invade France. And in the three following centuries all Germany's attacks were launched across it, as well as all the French invasions.

Both sides were anxious to secure their way through the plain of Lorraine. Later this no-man's-land, this attack route, became more than a strategic advantage and ranked as a rich prize in itself. In 1958 this coal-producing region was still economically dominated by France, but the German military authorities could still plaster the walls in the Saar with notices asking for forces volunteers, though the new recruits to the German army received their enlistment bounty in Saar francs—that is to say, in French francs. A semi-merger . . .

Germany maintained her cultural and sentimental links, while France took over everything else, provisionally at least. The fair-haired young men of the Saar dressed in Parisian style, and drove round in French cars, the 2 CV or the Déesse. France, for her part, provided a university and the inevitable Algerians. In the little electric tram which runs from Saarbrucken to Spiesen, through a valley still green and pleasant in spite of the mines, I have even seen a swarthy peddler of sheepskin rugs.

Ten months later, in June 1959, the tables were turned. Dresden china was ousting Sèvres and Limoges in the shops.

But, going back to September 1958 . . .

That Inauguration Day was a rainy Sunday. No one thought about iron-smelting or chains of customs posts that day. It rained continually and torrentially. The sky opened and water fell in foaming cataracts on dignitaries from Germany, France, Belgium, and the Saar alike, as they perched on the hillside in a morass of mud and grass. There were lots of Catholic priests, some Calvinist and Lutheran pastors, a rabbi, and an Orthodox priest . . .

Then there were the rest of the spectators, and the music societies from Belgium and the Saar. Never was rain endured with such good temper. The bonnets of the 'Scots of Courtrai' needed to be wrung out, just as if the gallant, musical company had reached their posts by swimming along their route up the Escaut, Rhine, and Saar rivers.

The Saar miners, dressed in coal-black suits with gold buttons, spat out from their trombones several pints of water for every few drops of music, and the Police Choral Society from Saarbrucken drank down the shower as they sang. Father Pire's white habit crossed the field, and floated on the wind of the storm right up on to the speaker's platform of a grandstand flanked by two cherry laurels. And still it rained on and on. Father Pire, holding his notes in one hand and an umbrella in the other, made his speech.

In a spirit of divine mischief, this Catholic priest borrowed some words of Luther for his opening sentence:

If the world should end tomorrow, I will still plant my little apple tree today.

By doing so, he no doubt wished to stress the bond of human brotherhood which unites all truly charitable hearts, irrespective of creeds and parties.

What should we do today in Europe for the cause of world peace? said Father Pire. While dreaming of universal peace, we will make a practical start by building a Europe of the Heart, and that is why we are planting a little apple tree here.

Our apple tree is this little, tiny village—the fifth European Village—which we have named after Albert Schweitzer, and for which all of you, my friends from so many different countries, will today share in laying the foundation stone. But what matter if it be small, so long as it is great in worth ? Together we shall have rescued twenty families, all with many children.

Here, my friends, the refugees will find a welcome awaiting them, and will be offered understanding and love. Is there anything on earth more wonderful and important to anyone than to be welcomed, understood, and loved ?

This village is certainly a very small apple tree. But is not one real apple tree, firmly planted and flourishing, better than a whole dream orchard ? You see, my friends, loving-kindness must find a practical expression. You can't love your fellow-man—the refugee, the invalid, the child—in the abstract, because people simply do not exist as abstract concepts. Love is for creatures of flesh and blood, for particular people, for this man, that woman, and their child. Small though the Albert Schweitzer village may be, it will consist of real men, real women, and real children whom we shall have rescued.

After that the foundation stone of the first house was laid, a heavy block of pink sandstone, and the European flag, with its twelve stars, was run up, while Beethoven's 'Hymn of Joy' streamed out over the valley. Underneath the stone was placed a Latin dedication on parchment, rolled up inside a copper cylinder:

'This day, Sunday the 21st September, 1958, a new European Village begins to rise from the ground at Spiesen. This Albert Schweitzer Village is being built by the Aid for Displaced Persons organization with the help of their friends throughout Europe, in order to restore to their uprooted brothers a home, work, friendship, and an opportunity to take root again in the good earth of a human community.'

A village? A hamlet, rather. The European Villages never number more than 150 inhabitants—that is to say, about twenty families. To have a larger number would run the risk of creating a ghetto, a feeling of being a tribe apart, for too many refugees concentrated in one place would turn back on themselves, impelled by habits acquired during the long years in camp. As it was, they would have to merge with the local population, and various precautions were taken to ensure this. For example, the houses were built by a local architect, so that the process of integration should begin with the setting.

A European Village is always built near a factory or works, for nine times out of ten the work offered to D.P.s is fairly light manual labour. For better or worse, that must obviously be the case.

Camp life makes a man rusty, and his former profession is often useless to him. This is the case with teachers and university professors, civil servants, and professional soldiers, and they have usually little physical strength remaining either. However, experience has shown that a very large percentage, as many as 80 per cent. of the population of the village, resume a normal life. Priority is always given to large families with many children, and in each family there must be at least one person able to work. In this way, the family circle is freed from the need to rely on the distributions of food parcels, clothing, and money, which are routine in the camps, a type of charity which often tends to give these poor people something of the mentality of beggars. The children attend school in the village with which the European hamlet is linked: they are often behind in their schooling and need to catch up, but their imperfect knowledge of their new country and its language makes their studies more difficult. Every effort is made to persuade the refugees and the people among whom they settle to forget their reciprocal prejudices and build up their mutual confidence in each other. The families must be brought back into circulation, for every European Village is not merely a matter of fulfilling a construction programme, it *means the complete reinstatement of its people as human beings.*

To achieve this is not so easy as it would seem. It is not just a question of bricks and mortar, and the re-housing of 150 people. Not at all, it is a whole process of re-education, for no one can live twelve years in a camp without bearing the marks of the experience. Even the best can stand no more than two years of this miasma of mind and heart that pervades these new ghettos of Europe, and is all the more sinister because there is no petrifying terror to accompany it. The prospect is no longer that of being killed, but of just not living . . .

In the camps, then, the D.P. gradually sinks to the sea floor, soon merges with the twilit depths, and achieves the kind of grey acceptance of existence which a dingy coral growth might have. He becomes panic-stricken at the idea of setting foot outside the camp, where he believes he would find himself in a completely strange world. He develops a fear of public spaces which only desperate souls can know.

This mental leprosy takes rapid hold, and the refugees from the Hungarian uprising of 1956 are as much affected as the 200,000 'old hands' left over from 1944. The work to be done in the villages is therefore prolonged, and needs both intelligence and patience: the building of houses through individual gifts, the purchase of furniture and household goods, finding suitable jobs for the able-bodied adults, arranging German lessons, instituting classes in their native tongue for the very little ones, forming scout troops, giving guidance through the social workers, organizing holidays.

As for money, that is found by Father Pire. Up till now 40,000,000 Belgian francs have been raised for the villages, but the most difficult thing is to open up the springs of goodwill, first of all among the people on the outside of the scheme. The 'powers that be' are distrustful, and the muni-

cipal bodies and the local population adopt a wait-and-see
attitude, which sometimes verges on hostility because they
do not understand our aims. There is very frequently opposition from the trade unions protecting the interests of the
unemployed in the neighbourhood, and from industrialists
who want to avoid trouble with the unions in employing
Stateless Persons. There is also the problem of the people
with misdirected good intentions. The offer to a student
just released from a santorium of a job as porter of sweet
cartons, when each case weighed sixty-six pounds, is a
classic example of this sort of goodwill. Finally, there are
the internal obstacles to the scheme. One has to create in
every village what the socialists would call a 'collective will
to live'. At the start, these families for whom the doors of
the normal world are opening are nothing but a collection
of unbalanced, demoralized misfits. They lack the unifying
link that only the combination of freedom and hope can
supply.

But, we must have patience . . .

Generally, all comes right again. The apathy of the D.P.
is an acquired, not an inborn, characteristic, and can be
banished by the touch of human sympathy. If we had ourselves lived for fourteen years in an Austrian camp, haunted
by frightful memories, surrounded by miserable wretchedness, dressed in the cast-off clothes of charity, and already
sunk in lassitude, we should probably be in very much the
same state.

These people, then, have to learn how to live again in the
new villages, how to paddle their own canoes again, and
have the chance to get their skill back in calm water. Their
benefactors must not try to do the paddling for them, must
not even want to. The will to manage by themselves is the
only real help they can have. One can only watch over
them, show them how to do it, and stay close at hand so
that they will not drown. It is hard for them at first, for

everything is new: regular work as father of a family, hav-
ing a separate houshold, going to school, and this terrible
necessity to make constant exercise of one's personal power
of decision. No more meals served at fixed times by the
camp bell! Some of them never manage to get used to it all
again. They are the real Hard Core . . .

But, it is a joy to watch the others taking root once more,
each of them rediscovering his own value as a person,
which is indeed infinite.

At Spiesen, it was only a foundation stone that had been
laid. What I wanted to see was a complete European Village
with all its people.

Father Pire took me to Bregenz, in Austria, not far from
Lake Constance, which he had founded in September 1956.
When I asked him the names of his hamlets he counted
them off on his fingers:

One : Aix-la-Chapelle, founded in May 1956.
Two : Bregenz, in Austria, September 1956.
Three : Augsburg, in Bavaria, May 1957
Four : Berchem-Sainte-Agathe, near Brussels, March 1958.
Five : Spiesen, in the Saar, September 1958.

And six, my Anne Frank Village at Wuppertal, May
1959 : I built it with the aid of both the Germans and the
Allies, both united in tribute to the memory of the little
Jewish girl who died in the hell of Bergen-Belsen when she
was only fourteen.

We were sitting in a meadow from which we could see
the colour-washed walls of the houses of the hamlet of
Bregenz—blue, pink, ochre, and white. The sun was shin-
ing, washing was flapping on the line, and in the distance
the mountains of the Tyrol shimmered in the warm haze.

NORTH SEA

HAMBURG

THE NETHERLANDS

BERLIN

BELGIUM · BRUSSELS

WUPPERTAL

AIX-LA-CHAPELLE

HUY

GERMANY

LUX

FRANKFURT

SPIESEN

SAARBRÜCKEN

METZ

STRASBOURG

AUGSBURG

MULHOUSE

MUNICH

BREGENZ

BERNE

SWITZERLAND

AUSTRIA

LYONS

MILAN

TURIN

ITALY

 1. *Aix - la - Chapelle.* First European Village, May 1956.

 2. *Bregenz.* Second European Village, September 1956.

 3. *Augsburg.* Third European Village, May 1957.

 4. *Berchem-Ste.-Agathe* (Brussels). The Nansen European Village, May 1958.

 5. *Spiesen.* The Albert Schweitzer Village, September 1958.

 6. *Wuppertal.* The Anne Frank Village. Foundation stone laid 31st May 1959.

They were expecting Father Pire, and there was a brave show of flags, archways covered with branches, speeches in his honour, house-to-house visits, and the presentation to him of all the babies. In the field where we were, some of the children were dancing to the sound of an accordion, while others were clustered round Father Pire's car, and later we were to find it covered all over with dusty little handprints. Near us the Austrian mayor was nodding his head in time to the music, his big soldier's moustache dancing a polka as he did so.

Every house, as I had seen, had its photograph of Father Pire. And now, as we stood before this blossoming human garden, the thread of confidence was once more renewed between us:

Father, you must be very happy.

Yes, I confess that I am. I am as happy as a gardener looking at his seedlings.

It is a moving sight, this new village set down in the midst of Europe. Has it occurred to you that there are no fences, either between the houses or alongside the road?

My refugees did not want them. But did you see the present the contractor made us?

No.

He gave each door a letter-box. That may not seem much to you, but to a D.P. it is a wonderful thing to have his own letter-box. It means he has an address, a home!

How happy and contented they all seem, and so much a part of the village! Look at those Austrian children who have come along to play with their little friends here.

Father Pire's eyes were shining, but suddenly his face clouded.

You think all this is fine don't you, he said, in a changed tone of voice, something quite normal, logical, and simple to achieve? Well, for all that, nothing is more painfully difficult than to replant men among others in a community. Everywhere it has been the same struggle. For instance, the introduction of Displaced Persons into the Saar, itself a land which is a kind of 'Displaced Country', caused no end of misgivings, created a sensation, in fact. There was the most violent opposition at the outset. An aggressive minority. confusing politics and charity, connected the European village with the scheme for a United Europe, rather a different proposition! The pro-German newspapers, or should I say the anti-French, came out with:
 'We have nothing in common with Europe.'
But explanations were given, and there was an about-turn on the subject. Today the entire Saar supports the Albert Schweitzer Village, and you saw at the Inauguration that Catholics, Orthodox, Jews, Calvinists, Lutherans, and Freemasons were all present. And also that crowd of agnostics, whom we ought to mention now and again! They all came, not for people of their own nationality, of their own religion, of their own blood, of their own culture, but for others. They united their efforts, joined in goodwill, in order that they might arrive by a thousand different paths in that country which every day becomes less inaccessible, Europe of the Heart.

You have spoken of difficulties, and here you all are on the best of terms. Wasn't there anything more than that rather silly comment in an insignificant newspaper?

Oh yes, indeed.

*At once he took from his case the files which he never
seems to be without. Many letters of gratitude, no doubt, as
well as letters showing complete lack of understanding.
Father Pire must reread these in the evening to cheer himself up.*

Listen to this: it's a letter I had while I was building my
village at Berchem-Sainte-Agathe, near Brussels: the Nansen Village:

Dear Father Pire,
     When I met a friend of mine who lives at Berchem-Sainte-
Agathe, and whom I interested some time ago in the Aid for
Displaced Persons, we got to talking of the Nansen Village. He
told me that although some of the local people would be either
sympathetic or else indifferent to the building of the village,
others regarded it with uneasiness, indeed hostility. One working man had declared: 'We might as well shut up shop when
they arrive.' One lady, in spite of having given to the Aid for
Displaced Persons fund, is not at all pleased to see them settled
near her, in her own community. The building contractors, the
architects and the landowners say that the presence of the village will lower land values and the tone of the town and sur-
rounding district. Among business people and in the shops, my
friend and his wife have often heard comments expressive of
disquiet, mistrust, and even antagonism. But maybe you know
all about this, and perhaps the same thing has happened with
earlier European Villages.
     But, just in case, I thought I should warn you, hoping it may
be of help to the Aid to Displaced Persons organization. Every
time he has had the chance, my friend has tried to counter all
this, but he has gone carefully because, even though he is himself completely won over and quite willing that D.P.s should
be settled near his property, it is impossible just the same to
guarantee in advance with absolute certainty that they will behave in the sort of way which will banish every fear and mis-
giving voiced by 'the opposition'.

Well, what do you think of that?

I think it is not so much out of the usual run of human behaviour? Did you find the same kind of reaction in Germany?

When I started work on my first village, at Aix-la-Chapelle, the mayor commented: 'Here comes Father Pire with his anti-social misfits!' The day after we laid the foundation stone of the village at Bregenz, the mayor wrote to tell me that the council of the little town near which we were building required the erection of a seven-foot-high wall all round the village. The local people are afraid that they will otherwise have all their apple trees stripped, he said. When we started work on the third village, at Augsburg, someone wrote to the mayor saying, 'If this gypsy camp (and by that he meant my beautiful European Village) is set up in our town, it will be over your dead body.' In one little Swiss town the council refused to allow the opening of a home for aged refugees because 'it would mean enlarging the cemetery'.

When the D.P.s actually arrived these prejudices were dissipated. The native residents could see the sort of people they had to do with and realized that no one was asking, either that they should accept the D.P.s as indistinguishable from themselves, or that the D.P.s should try to become so. Why ask a Rumanian to turn into a Belgian, or a Czech turn into a Saarlander? It is enough that they should be able to reintegrate themselves slowly as part of a human community, that the ghetto complex be banished and the status of respected minority take its place.

Like that we have no more Stateless Persons sitting on their luggage in the station, and waiting for a train that will never come?

Not any longer. In my Villages we have human beings

settled in their own homes, paying their own rent, eating
bread won by the sweat of their own brow, buying their
own radios and motor-cycles, and who, after having un-
packed their luggage, hang on their walls their icons and
pictures of their parents, and photos of their old country
houses or little farms. Two years after the settlement of the
refugees a degree of integration is reached which would
have seemed impossible a few months before their arrival, as
that letter from Brussels shows. Let's go and have a look at
Aix-la-Chapelle, you'll find the people there very much
like you and me. Certainly they aren't angels, but you do
not come across angels on this earth nowadays, there are
only men. And men are always both wonderful and disappointing. Talking about sin, Pascal called it 'the misfortune
of a great nobleman come down in the world', and my great
noblemen who have come down in the world do, like the
rest of us, the best they can. And we mustn't exact from
them the kind of heroic standards we should never dream
of expecting from ourselves.

*And now, Father, we come to the question of the refugees
leaving for the Villages, the choosing of the 'elect'?*

Considering the countless number of D.P.s the need to
make such a choice would seem dramatic, he replied, but
no one is ever confronted with the refugees *en masse*, it is
only in the mind's eye that they ever appear like that. We
must keep on the practical level, using ordinary human
means, poor though human means may be.

How then do you choose?

It is most frequently the godmother or godfather of a
D.P. who pleads his cause, or else it may be a camp social
worker who brings an interesting case to our notice.

What makes a case 'interesting'?

Where there is an instance of a family with children. Those tens of thousands of children growing up in the camps are an obsession with me. We try to rescue the large families, or those in which the breadwinner has suffered from tuberculosis, thus preventing the emigration of them all and ending their hopes of integration in a new community. At Bregenz we have a Russian family to whom a ninth child was born only a few months back, and in the same village we have a young Yugoslav widow with her nine children, a Hungarian family with six, and a Ukrainian woman with another six.

In the village at Augsburg we have two Polish families with six children apiece. Similarly, the little baby whom so many people will have seen photographed in my arms, is the sixth child of a Polish family living at the Village of Aix-la-Chapelle.

But I suppose the number of children is not your only criterion?

No. I must take into account their ability to adapt themselves. The refugee and his new country must be in harmony. For example, it is easier to get a Pole to take root again in Belgium than in Germany. Every refugee coming from the East wants to get as far from the Iron Curtain as possible, or at least to be in a country which has a reputation for standing up to the Russians.

Next, I must have people who have really given up the idea of emigrating to America. What a mirage of the Promised Land emigration to America is for these people! As if one did not have to work as hard over there as here! If I only took those with emigration in mind, my villages would be nothing but waiting-rooms.

Then, I must take into account the firmness of their resolution to give up being half-way to beggars, something made so easy by the distribution of parcels.

Finally, the D.P.s must have a genuine wish to settle in a Village .

But, surely, they all want that.

Unfortunately, no. Many no longer wish to leave the camp, or to have to exert themselves. In a Village people have to earn their own living, pay their rent, do their own cooking. 'It's too much trouble,' thinks the D.P. who has grown used to vegetating and has, so to speak, lost his pride. So, I have to find those who have their self-respect, and if they have enough, I win. If their habit of begging is stronger than their self-respect, I lose. In any case, whatever the choice to be made, I have to take a chance.

If I only accepted people of whom I was completely sure, I should never take anyone! And even if all the rules of selection are followed, disappointment can still lie in wait. I have known instances when a camp commandant would warmly recommend really antisocial types.

But why?

To get rid of them, that's all.

Has a D.P. ever been sent back to camp after having left to settle in a Village?

Once, I believe. It was a poor woman who was quite incapable of making her new home anything else but a camp, and in three months it was in a frightful state. She paid no

more heed to her children than she did to her household
duties, and couldn't even cook. She had to be sent back to
Austria, and that seems to suit her very well. The social
workers look after her children, while she awaits the dinner
bell, and free hand-outs of tobacco. She had turned her
house into a gypsy caravan, and was a true Bohemian!

*Did the idea of a European Village spring up in your mind
complete, just as you have carried it out?*

No, I hesitated, feeling my way, and I went off at first on
completely the wrong tack. It was in 1954, when I was only
concerning myself with sponsorships and the old people. I
was racking my brains as to how we could help the other
D.P.s to become real human beings again, and to begin
with, I was taken with the silly idea of bettering camp conditions on a permanent basis. I would have made the camps
more human, done some repainting, had the walls papered,
cleaned them up generally, and introduced social services.
But this would only have been gilding the bars of the cage,
and, anyway, the Nations were not at all anxious to see the
camps made permanent.

Then I thought of buying a house in Austria, gathering a
group of elderly D.P.s there, and building some greenhouses
where they could cultivate early vegetables. But that would
have been just tinkering with the problem. Still, I must admit that I have always liked tinkering with things. Once,
I took to breeding Angora rabbits at the monastery
of La Sarte. Lord, how unpredictable those animals
were, and how their valuable pelts made the good fathers
sneeze!

Anyway, I did not at once give up the idea of a working
community, and I thought of those 'ghost' villages you find
in the south of France, where the population has moved
elsewhere. This was another fairy-tale idea, we should have

just settled there and the soil would have producd crops all by itself! But running a community involves the employment of labour, investment of capital, creation of a sales service, and you only need one crook to break up the group. And so I came round to the idea of doing the building of the houses myself, and getting work on the spot for my villagers.

How happy you must have felt the day you laid the foundation stone of the first Village?

Happy, but annoyed, too!

It was on 6th May 1956 at Aix-la-Chapelle. I had made myself familiar with all the arrangements, and foreseen everything: order of precedence for the dignitaries, the little place cards, and drawing-pins to affix the cards to the chairs on the platform. The sorting out of all these problems of etiquette and human vanity had taken me hours, and I felt so proud of myself. Perhaps that was why the good God punished me: the chairs were metal ones, which would not take drawing-pins and the wind scattered half my cards. A cardinal and one of the bishops felt themselves slighted. They were already out of temper, therefore, before we came to the banquet, and when they found—or thought they did—that they were once more allotted inferior places, they went to dine in a restaurant.

But, listen to this! On the day before a woman had gone into a bank in Brussels, and when they asked, 'Can I help you?' she said: 'I want to do something towards healing the wounds of war. Give me the account number of a suitable charity!'

By chance the bank manager knew of the Aid for Displaced Persons organization, and two telephone calls later the pockets of the D.P.s were enriched to the tune of twelve million French francs. One thing compensates for another . . .

They were calling us now to show us the babies. In the garden of a home nearby, a man was planting roses. He happily waved his cap, and his wife wanted to kiss Father Pire's hand, as is the custom in Central Europe. Further on, and further on again, indeed everywhere, people were waiting to thank him, but he was embarrassed and rather tried to escape their homage.

Are you shy, Father, or are you just tired?

Neither, he whispered, but at times like these I think of what St. Vincent de Paul said to a little sister who was going out to visit the poor for the first time :

'Never forget that it is you who are beholden to them. See to it that you have their forgiveness for the good you do them.'

And he took a baby in his arms.

These are the ones who most touch my heart, he said. In my office I have a photograph of the first child born in my first Village. Without me, he would have made his debut in the world in a camp. I have seen to it that he was born free.

He gave the child back to its mother, asking: 'What's his nationality?'

'Oh, he's a European!' she answered Father Pire triumphantly.

CHAPTER FOURTEEN

───────────◆───────────

The Nobel Peace Prize

HE WAS SITTING on a bundle of newspapers, moist from the press—not the best thing to do in a pure white Dominican habit, but his office was full of them. This was a complete edition of Hard Core, the journal of the Aid for Displaced Persons Organization, of which each issue runs to 80,000 copies.

For a dozen years Father Pire has distributed them free to patrons of his work. He would have liked to buy an addressing machine, but it would have cost 100,000 Belgian francs and, in his hatred of excessive administration expenditure, he was horrified, as one would expect. Since then, a thousand Belgian children, the pupils of two boarding schools have addressed them by hand, and not a single one has ever thought of his eighty lines as an 'imposition'.

Father Pire genially offered me an armchair—five bundles of papers—and before I could ask a single question had sped straight back to the year, the month and the day at which we had broken off. It was in 1953, a significant year, since it was then that he was able to give up his duties as curé, and devote himself entirely to his work.

His Dominican superiors were quite agreeable to his doing so, and the secular clergy were highly delighted. For their part, they had long been exasperated, not so much at having to control a curé who assumed so many duties, but at hav-

ing to admit that he carried them all out scrupulously, without giving the slightest just cause for criticism. In the ecclesiastical world, as in the lay, there are sometimes gentlemen like this, who are quite distressed at having faultless colleagues.

It was no good asking Father Pire to elaborate on points such as these. If he had ever been conscious of it all, he had forgotten now, but the little town of Huy had a longer memory. They treasure there the memory of the triumphant reception they gave to the Nobel Peace Prize Winner six years later to wipe out the recollection of certain former disagreements between them. Once upon a time, hadn't they wanted to teach Father Pire how to manage his charities efficiently?

I suppose you were able to sit back and relax now, Father? Irony tinged my voice as I asked the question, and he replied in the same tone.

Naturally I didn't have much to do now that I wasn't *curé* of La Sarte any more. I just had to find the money to keep my four old people's homes going, keep an eye on fifteen thousand sponsorships, bring out the *Hard Core* regularly, make thrice-yearly tours of the camps, deal with thousands of letters, carry on with my activities for the young people, hear confessions, try to help no end of people, and give lectures over half Europe. Then, there were my duties as a Dominican, to say Mass, read my breviary, tell my beads, see my colleagues, practise daily meditation, observe the monastic rule of silence and the fasts, account to my superiors for all my actions, and ask their permission for this, that and the other. And, of course, to sleep a little sometimes. A while later, I started to build my villages.

Tell the truth, now! You are never happy unless you are working yourself to death.

That is true, I suppose. I have sometimes compared my life to a stream which grows little by little as it flows, but keeps on its course. I get impatient if the current lessens speed, and that did happen once. I started dreaming immediately of setting out for Korea as a chaplain.

We have been following the stream, Father, but now we have reached the estuary—the award to you in 1958 of the Nobel Peace Prize. There you were quietly irrigating your little valley, and suddenly you were transformed to a great river, a sea, an ocean! The morning after the announcement, a Belgian journalist put in a nutshell what had happened when he wrote of you:

'Henceforth, you are part and parcel of every man's dreams for peace.' Won't you tell me how you came to win the Nobel Prize?

Oh, it was all very simple, and rather amusing, too, as it happens.

In October 1956 I was at home ill in Dinant, being looked after by my parents, when the Hungarian revolt suddenly broke out, and the first refugees arrived in Belgium a few days later, at Huy, to be exact. I was ashamed to be ill at such a time. I couldn't resign myself to doing nothing for them, but I had no money, and so I wrote to the great World Foundations, though with no very clear idea as to whether they concerned themselves with charity or not. I wrote to the Ford Foundation, the Rockefeller Foundation and the Nobel Foundation. The replies were firmly in the negative, but written with a clear conscience : 'We have already given time and again to many different causes.'

Among the replies was one pointing out that the Nobel Funds were not in any case available because they were combined in a prize awarded for work towards Peace, and that this Nobel Peace Prize was awarded not by Sweden, but by Norway. It also told me that anyone who felt he had deserved the prize, should send a report of his activities to the Norwegian Parliament, the *Storting*, before 1st February.

I had a fairly clear recollection of how the great Nobel had bequeathed his native country a fortune made in dynamite and destined to promote peace among mankind, but I had to do a little research before I understood why Sweden referred me to Norway. After Nobel's death in 1896, Scandinavia developed politically in a way which led to the division of the peninsula between the two countries in 1905, and all their goods, both spiritual and temporal, were also divided at the same time. This applied to the Nobel Foundation as well, so Sweden still awards the prizes for Science and Literature, but Norway chooses each year the winner of the Nobel Peace Prize. The actual choice is in the hands of the Norwegian Parliament, or rather of a special parliamentary commission which works in full agreement with the Foundation and is composed of the country's highest authorities in matters of ethics. I need hardly say that these people study a case and make their judgment with complete impartiality, never allowing themselves to be influenced by public opinion, or by philosophical, religious, or political consideratons. The Nobel Foundation's methods of inquiry are extremely thorough, and have some unusual features. Actually, the candidates do not present themselves, but must be presented by someone who, either by the office he holds or his intrinsic merit, is obviously a person well qualified to speak. There is a list of people holding suitable offices, in which ministers and members of parliaments throughout the world occupy a conspicuous place, and former Nobel prize-winners are also included.

I showed the letter to a friend of mine, Monsieur Fernand Dehousse, President of the Council of Europe, explaining to him that I needed money for the refugees, and that I believed I was right in thinking that the Nobel prize amounted to a considerable sum.

'Let's take a chance!' he said.

And so you sent in a report?

No, but I sent a booklet summarizing my efforts, a straightforward prospectus I had had printed some time before. I even forgot to send a covering letter with it, and in the end my friend Fernand Dehousse wrote by express to the Norwegian *Storting*.

Why by express?

Because there had been a little delay, and it was not till 30th January that we suddenly realized that the closing date for the candidacies was the 31st. The *Storting* sent us the prescribed form and we filled it in, and I went on with my work. That year—it was 1957—the prize went to Lester Pearson, Canada's Minister for Foreign Affairs. All the same, and I only tell you this because it is true, people were beginning to talk about me, or rather, I think it was the refugees who were beginning to get themselves talked about. Towards the end of the year, someone coming back from Oslo said to me mysteriously:

'You have put a good many lock-gates behind you, but what an extraordinary thing, to send a leaflet instead of a report! You'll have to get a really full one prepared.'

According to the rules of procedure, such a report must be submitted by the Government of the country to which the candidate belongs.

My helpers drew up our report in the December of 1957 and sent it off to the Belgian Government. It went astray in their offices; no one realized it was missing until the 15th January 1958, when I was asked for copies of it, and so, for a second time, Father Pire's memorandum just arrived in Norway on 30th January, at the last moment! And that's all there was to it.

He laughed, and so did I, though not for the same reason. In fact, he had committed a grave sin of omission. He had not told me all, just out of native reserve and reticence of soul! Or was he really trying, after all, to hide something from me? But, it was not impossible that this pure-hearted man, this ingenuously charitable soul, had not realized right until the last moment why Mr. Otto Kildal, the Norwegian ambassador in Brussels, had suddenly interested himself in the Aid for Displaced Persons organization.

On the 31st March the foundation stone of Nansen Village had been laid at Berchem-Sainte-Agathe.

Among the diplomats present at the ceremony, 'one observed', as the glossy weeklies would say, Mr. Otto Kildal. Or, more accurately, 'one had not observed', for that was all that apparently happened: absolute—and diplomatic— silence. However, a certain diplomatic bag shuttled to and fro between Brussels and Oslo, stuffed with information on the Homes, the sponsorships, and the European Villages. All part of the procedure, no doubt!

They say that at some time between April and September 1958, Father Pire was invited to dinner one evening at the Norwegian Embassy. Only a few guests were present, elderly Norwegians, grave, dignified and silent, who listened thoughtfully to the Dominican monk and looked at him consideringly, as they warmed a glass of precious, anise-flavoured brandy in the hollow of their hands. Brandy which had splashed about for six months in oaken casks, twice crossing the Line in the hold of a cargo vessel from Bergen or Trondheim.

They spoke of everything but the Nobel Prize, and Father Pire went back to Huy pretty well convinced that he had taken his final examination. The elderly gentlemen, members of the Nobel Foundation, had come specially from Oslo to look him over, and all that remained was the public ordeal.

He was invited to Oslo by the Norwegian section of the European Movement. On 21st October 1958, in the Aula, or Great Hall of the University, he quite simply gave an account of what he was doing and why. It was a moving story, and his speech was an outstanding one.

Outside the clear, frosty night was coating the last leaves of the lime-trees with rime. Oslo was asleep by the side of its fjord which sparkled with stars, all her double doors and windows secured in place for the winter. It was the first sleep of the long Northern night. But here in the great marble hall, there was life and profound attention.

Up on the rostrum there was the white robe of the Dominican Order: Father Pire was addressing his Norwegian audience. He had come over from Belgium, not to give a lecture, but because the route of his crusade for brotherhood among men happened to lead him there. He knew that in Norway, perhaps more than elsewhere, people have a sense of what is just and that what they believe often flowers in practice, in the carrying out of social projects. He knew that the Norwegians combine a deep love of independence with a conviction that it is a duty to co-operate with all free peoples in establishing universal peace.

Father Pire gathered his thoughts as he stood at the rostrum. In the simplicity of his apostolic spirit he was about to say such things as these Northmen had rarely heard. There among the crowd facing him was the King of Norway who, after having granted him a lengthy private audience in the afternoon, had wished to hear him speak in the evening. Beside the King sat a young girl, Princess Astrid.

Behind the first three rows of guests of honour, the Norwegian people had taken their places, interested in this Cru-

sade bound to no religion or party, but fired only by a burning idea of compassion.

They crowded in. Ordinarily the University hall is only a third full, even for an outstanding concert, but this evening there wasn't a vacant place. Yet, all they were going to hear was a tale of infinite hardships and desperate struggles.

Nervously, Father Pire collected his thoughts. He was going to unfold before these silent men of the North, with their slow, considered ways of making up their minds, his great scheme for the Anne Frank Village which he wanted built by the combined efforts of the Germans and the Allied Resistance. He was nervous because he knew how sternly sensitive the Norwegians still were on the subject of the Occupation, how in certain parts of Europe the members of the Resistance were still implacably hostile, and how many millions of Germans had memories that were either too long or too short.

In conclusion, after giving an account of his work, he said:

In my secret heart I hope that the sixth European Village will bear the name of a little girl, a fourteen-year-old Jewish child who died in the concentration camp at Belsen. Why did Anne Frank die, and what lesson did her death teach us? My conscience has supplied an answer, and it is this: in 1958, fourteen years after the end of the war, those who were once allies must join with those who were once their enemies in building the Anne Frank European Village. There are so many barriers separating mankind, one of them being enduring resentment, but Anne Frank belongs to the whole world, Germans as much as members of the Resistance.

Every day in these past fourteen years children have been born, and can't their parents, whether German or Allied, make a generous gesture in the spirit of Europe of the Heart? This sixth European Village, the Anne Frank Village, would not be spoken of as the Village of Reconciliation—that would be too weakly negative—but rather as the Village of New-found Brotherhood, the Village of the Outstretched Hand, the Village of Peace.

And it is not at Belsen, where Anne died, that I would want to build my sixth European Village . . .

As he finished speaking, the audience applauded Father Pire long and loud, and then filed out in silence. One could feel that the words of the speaker had set the scales of judgement atremble in the minds of these Northern beings, with their calm assurance which is sometimes a little remote from the direct impact of humanity's distress. But . . .

Actually, it was in Norway that Father Pire hoped to build the Anne Frank Village, but it was not to be. He learnt that in Oslo—vanitas vanitatum—on the morning after the solemn presentation to him of the Nobel Prize. The village is now being built at Wuppertal[1] in Germany, and the Norwegians have contributed one hundred thousand crowns towards it.

Father, the Nobel Prize was awarded at the beginning of November 1958. What were you doing between 22nd October and 9th November?

On my way back from Oslo, I passed through Brussels and went on to Corsica, to make a retreat. When I got there, I found in my mail a Norwegian press cutting, with a French translation, which said that the Nobel Prize would not be awarded that year, or that if it were, it would be the reward of the work of some institution, some group effort. I had thought as much. That would be the end of it as far as I was concerned. I was weary of reports and inquiries, and had

Inaugurated 31st May 1959.

absolutely no intention of starting all over again the next year.

Returning to La Sarte monastery in the early days of November, I began, on the eighth to preach to a retreat. There were about thirty people taking part, down in the little guest house at the bottom of the garden. On the second day one of my secretaries had me called into the parlour of the monastery : I had to sign a few things. As we worked we talked, of nothing in particular and of everything under the sun—that is to say, we talked of life in general. And I found myself saying :

'The Nobel Prize could have brought me only one fundamental benefit : confidence in myself through others confidence in me.'

'Even the Nobel Prize could not give that sort of confidence,' said my secretary; 'that is only gained by meditation, and cultivation of one's inward life.'

That was at about half-past one. At two the retreat began again. We formed a circle and discussion on education started, with a big speech made by a small young lady. The room was divided in two by a red velvet curtain and when I heard footsteps on the other side I confess I thought someone was eavesdropping. 'Who is there?' I said, rather sharply, but when the curtain parted it was the startled, smiling face of a Dominican, Brother Xhaufflaire, that appeared.

'Father,' he said, 'they want you to go down to your office in the Rue du Marché at once.'

It would have to be something serious to interrupt a retreat in this way. Had there been an accident, I thought, a fire? From the porter's lodge I telephoned my secretary.

'Father,' said Mademoiselle Jolling, 'I can't be sure whether it isn't a practical joke, but the Associated Press say they urgently want an interview. They claim that you've been awarded the Nobel Prize.'

'Impossible,' I replied. 'It's just another hoax.'

It was now three o'clock, and I had only mentioned it in passing to the Father Prior, but I was curious, and a quarter of an hour later I telephoned my office again. 'It must be true,' they said this time, 'the telephone never stops ringing and we have already had a congratulatory telegram.'

At that time you still hadn't received any official notification then?

No. What had happened was this. The Nobel Foundation had wired from Oslo that morning, but my address had been badly written, and instead of going to Huy, the telegram went to Huyse, a village in Flanders.

From there, it was sent back to the Central Office marked 'Unknown', and it didn't finally get to Huy until half-past four. The message asked me to hold back the news until seven o'clock, but Radio-Luxembourg had announced it at four. In short, all the world knew I was a Nobel Prizewinner, except me.

I went back to the young people of my discussion group, and the moment I appeared one of the girls called out to me : 'Is it the Nobel Prize ?'

I nodded, and there was a burst of applause from them all. It was tremendously moving.

Then I went down to my office and the flood burst its banks. I received the reporters and newsmen for five solid hours, and at seven-thirty I heard interviews with me on the radio which had only ended a quarter of an hour before.

What did they ask you?

Always the same things. 'How much is the prize, and what are you going to do with it ?'

And . . . and how much was it?

Two hundred and fifteen thousand kroner, about £15,000 or $45,000.

Were there any odd incidents?

Oh yes. Several weeks later I gave an interview to an American journalist who suggested we lunch at a restaurant. My small appetite surprised him, but it was my choice of menu that threw him into consternation. I wouldn't have caviare, and he kept on saying in a stupefied, disconcerted and pitying tone:
'What? You've just won the Nobel Prize and you won't buy yourself caviare?' He almost despised me.

Weren't your family pleased?

Can't you imagine it! But there were no elaborate speeches. One might even say that my mother wasn't all that pleased.

Really?

Oh yes. You see, one paper had told my life story and said that I was fifty, although I was still only forty-nine. But, in a month's time my parents were due to celebrate their fiftieth anniversary, their golden wedding.
'Married fifty years and with a son fifty years old,' grumbled my mother. 'What on earth will people think!'

I've no need to ask if you received many messages of congratulation.

Thousands, and I replied to them all. Those letters were

filled with such a radiant warmth of friendship and were so comforting . . .

Many sent money as well to help my work. It came in from everywhere. An old peasant woman living somewhere north of Trondheim sent me fifteen Norwegian crowns. She had caught sight of one of the hens in her chicken-run standing on one leg by the wire-netting 'with the miserable look of a D.P.' and it had put her in mind of me.

You must have had begging letters, too?

Yes. Sometimes they were very touching, and I tried to reply helpfully, but there were others which were very amusing. One of the very first letters I had came by express from Sweden. It accompanied a box of cough lozenges, and said : 'All Nobel Prizewinners use our lozenges. Please be so good as to send us a few words confirming that you find them effective.'

Were they any good?

I never let them know, even at the risk of breaking a tradition.

Were you asked any odd questions?

A few. Generally speaking, the Anglo-Saxon journalists were much more interested in my height and weight, and the colour of my eyes, than in my European Villages. One of them even took a tape-measure from his pocket and carefully measured me from top to toe and round the middle ! Still, once they had quenched their thirst for 'vital statistics' they were kindly and understanding.

How many letters did you get altogether?

I don't really know. We stopped counting and just weighed them instead. Many were addressed in the most extraordinary way.

Father Pire took out from one of his chests (his office is fitted up like a naval officer's) a great brown file and opened it. A shower of envelopes fell out.

They came from the four corners of the world, he said, and the oddest thing about them is the fact that they ever reached me. Look at the way they are addressed : all the confiding trust, the uncertainty and muddleheadedness of our little human souls is there ! My employees picked out the best of them and when I am overburdened with worry, I take down my brown file. It's a splendid remedy. Shall we try it ?

First of all there were ten different ways of spelling the name Huy, the seat of the Aid for Displaced Persons organization:

Huy, Huit, Huik, Hui, Huix, Huitz, Nuit, Huisme, Oui— or more simply still: 8. Then came the bewildering, and sometimes touching, series of ways of addressing Father Pire, from which I made a wonderful anthology. All these letters were meant for him, but Belgian postmen must all be experts in cipher to have realized it.

One correspondent wasn't going to give anything away, even on the envelope, which just read:

Mister.

Another went a little farther and put:

Mister X.

Someone else absent-mindedly confused Father Pire and his secretary:

Reverend Father Jolling.

And yet another reversed the procedure:

Miss Dominique Pire.

Many put great faith in the Post Office, for one envelope from Germany read simply:

To the Dominican monk, Father Pire, Belgium.

Some were respectful:

The Reverend Canon Pire; His Lordship, Bishop of the Displaced Persons; His Eminence, Father Pire; The Honourable Reverend Pastor Pire; The Reverend Senior Pastor Pire; The Most Reverend, the Great Philanthropist, Father Pire; His Lordship Georges Pire; The Most Excellent P. Pire, the Great Belgian Prizewinner for Humanitarianism; His Dominican Eminence, Georges Pire of Belgium; The Most Esteemed R. P. Pire—all this in a motley of torques, French, German, and Italian.

And the ways they found to spell his name:

Father Pierre; Father Pier; Father Père; Father Pir; Father Pyr; Father Bie; Father Peer; . . . even Father Riverbank, in reference to his broadcast talks in which he spoke of himself as being like a river.

There were those who had heard D.P.s or Displaced Persons spoken of, and one of these boldly wrote to the:

198

P.D. Society, Huy.

Someone else had a very bad memory and just wrote to:

The Reverend Father——

A writer with a poetical turn wrote to:

The Fountainhead of Aid to Displaced Persons.

A reader of the D.P. magazine wrote to:

The Reverend Father of the Hard Core.

This one was very precise:

The Reverend Father Pire of the Order of Aid to Stateless Persons.

A radio listener wrote:

The Emigrant Aid Scheme of the Reverend Father of the Radio.

A Greek gave minute directions:

By Personal Express Registered Post—The Reverend Father Georges Pire, monk of the Catholic Church in Belgium, who has received a Nobel Prize.

Here is one from someone who had forgotten the right address, and, since it was the year of the World Exhibition at Brussels, sent his letter to the Central Organization responsible for arranging tourist accommodation:

To the Logexpo Office, for the Reverend Priest Georges Pir, Protector of the Refugees.

Someone rather nervous confused Father Pire's name with 'peur'—fear, and wrote to:

The Organizers of the Fear.

There were lots who wrote as they heard, more or less, and when people talked to them of the Aid for Displaced Persons organization, it led them to put on their envelopes:

The Aid for People who have Come Down in the World.
 • (Aide aux Personnes déclassés.)

Or:

The Aid for Moveable People.
   (Aide aux Déplaçants.)

Or again:

The Assistance for the Lonely.
   (Assistance aux Isolés.)

And even:

The Being at the Displaced Persons Organization.
   (L'Etre aux Personnes Déplacées.)

And this, which isn't very kind:

The Ugly Woman at the Displaced Persons Organization
   (Laide aux Personnes Déplacées.)

There were some who gave him official titles:

His Excellency Director Pire, Manager of the Displaced Persons Establishment; His Grace the Director of Displaced People.

Some who touched the heart:

To the Abandoned Children.
    (Ausen fant abant donné.)

Coming from Stuttgart, but no doubt written by an Irish emigré was one addressed to:

Mr. O'Pire.

And it must have been a fine big fellow with a healthy appetite who called him:

Reverend Father Poupart.[1]

And someone who didn't see Father Pire on a very large scale who wrote to:

His Grace the little Abbé.

One of the nicest, just to bring up the rear:

The Reverend Dominican Father—Father Pire of Operation 'Little Streams'—Father Pire, the Friend of Young and Old.

And lastly, one which he well deserved:

Reverend Father Pire, Nobel Prizewinner of the Heart.

[1] Edible crab.

*We both laughed, but not for long. Father Pire raised a
warning finger:*

Never forget that these very envelopes came to me either
filled with a tale of distress, or crammed with offers of goodwill and friendship.

And he closed the brown file once more.

*And now let us go back to the ceremonies at Oslo! The
Nobel Foundation had fixed the 10th December 1958 for the
presentation of the prize.*

*'Peace on earth and goodwill to all men.' When Father
Pire arrived by the Nord Express that Monday morning, he
found the city in the midst of its preparations for the Feast
of the Nativity. The Northern twilight sparkled. In the
public squares the illuminated Christmas trees were reflected in the myriad crystals of the new-fallen snow. The
Nobel Peace Prize had certainly dropped into the sack of
Father Christmas.*

*On the broad wooden platforms of Oslo station a Belgian
and Norwgeian reception committee was awaiting the
prizewinner's arrival, and schoolchildren were everywhere.
These young Norwegians, fair youthful giants with rosy
cheeks, swathed in woollens and wearing wellingtons, could
be seen calmly charging through the week-end crowds, kick-
ing up hail-storms of trodden snow or splashing up glorious
showers of black slush. They went along like machines, just
as powerful and innocent of evil intent: admirable, but one
got out of their way as if they were bulldozers.*

*As the Nord Express came in there was a moment of per-
plexity. This fine train is actually entitled to a special double
platform, one on each side, and while the reception committee waited on the right-hand platform some mischievous*

chance led Father Pire to alight on the left. Happily, matters were soon sorted out. Under fire from the photographers, whose flashlights were as blinding as the polar dawn was glimmeringly uncertain, Father Pire gazed about him unable to take anything in, and had for a start to join battle with the agile Norwegian journalists, with their astrakhan and sheepskin hats. Swifter-moving than the diplomats and the venerable heads of the Nobel Foundation, they hurled themselves towards the door of the Prizewinner's carriage, leaping over luggage trolleys and heaps of snow on the way.

Father Pire smiled, bowed, smiled again, and at last received the official congratulations. How did he reply? If you think he made a formal reply, or gave them a few polite phrases, or improvised a hasty speech, you do not know the prizewinner very well. No. Immediately on alighting after two days and a night on the train, bareheaded in the piercing Northern cold, standing in the snow and with frozen hands, Father Pire was pursuing his inward dream and his outer work of brotherly charity, and questioned his friendly helpers.

Was everything in order? Had a time-table of interviews and periods for dictating replies to his mail been arranged? Not a second was to be lost. Invited to Oslo to receive the homage of the Norwegian nation and of men of goodwill the world over, Father Pire was thinking only of his Anne Frank Village, the new town he was preparing for the refugees.

While they were honouring his work, he was getting on with doing it.

And now he was in the town. His seminarist's suitcase and a whole arsenal of printed matter had been loaded on to the Belgian Ambassador's car, and he was on his way to the cosy drawing-rooms of the Embassy, the Royal Palace, and official honours.

His nose to the window, Father Pire looked at the illuminations, the giant Christmas tree in front of the Univer-

sity, its boughs loaded with apples of light, and the candles, taller than the street lamps, planted along the pavements and streaming out flames of oil.

What was he thinking about, this man who, within two minutes of receiving the telegram announcing the prize, had already devoted two million Belgian francs to the completion of the Nansen Village at Berchem-Sainte-Agathe and the building of the Anne Frank Village?

He was counting off on his figures to remind himself to (1) Finish off some work for the Anne Frank Village, (2) Buy some little souvenir for his mother, (3) Try to find some coloured pictures of boats for a sick child in Belgium who adores them and can't wait for him to get back with them.

And after that? Ah yes, after that, there was the Nobel Prize.

On the first day of his visit it had been dark, foggy, and damp, but the next morning Oslo crackled with frost, and sparkled on the shore of her bay like a diamond on blue velvet. There was not one Father Pire in the city, but ten, twenty, fifty, he packed so much into every hour. Helping him were his friends from Huy, his Provincial, his Prior, his secretary Mademoiselle Jolling, and his good and kindly adviser, the wise Mr. Kildal, Norwegian Ambassador in Brussels, for whom the award of the Nobel Prize had not only meant the satisfaction of a duty done, but a measure of diplomatic triumph. Then there was Monsieur de Bois, the Belgian Ambassador to Oslo, who had worked in his cause long and assiduously. And he had his Norwegian friends, thinking of them all, even to the most humble. In the midst of his grandeur, the winner of the Nobel Peace Prize would want to assemble the embassy staff, from the chancellor to the meanest scullion, to thank them for their warm-hearted support.

For the dignified and splendidly appointed mansion where

the Belgian Ambassador lived had been put at Father Pire's service. At his command, the furniture, the tables and chairs disappeared, moved to one side or re-grouped themselves according to press conference requirements. All the Oslo reporters were there, and all the photographers, and all the newsreel men, moving the torrid zone of their searchlights here and there.

One black-and-white artist devoted himself to turning the prize-winner into a handsome film-star type, but at the end of the sitting Father Pire, who is not above a little innocent malice, showed him one of the caricatures made of him in Belgium: it gave him an enormous nose and a chin like a sabot. The artist, a man of delicate refinement, was stupefied at the sight and not a little vexed. But he was not the only one who wanted to make Father Pire conform in every way to people's preconceived notions.

What didn't they invent to say about the good Dominican! It was his simplicity that disconcerted them. Again and again poor Father Pire repeated to the pressmen that he was very pleased about it, and he hoped that the award of the Nobel Prize would attract attention to the fate of the refugees, but all that was not the sort of thing to assuage the thirst of these inquirers. And so they made things up, though this happened less in Norway than in Belgium, and less there than in France. Among those who visited him in November, there was someone who claimed to have seen Father Pire, his features convulsed with emotion, his eyes red with tears and riveted to the sky, fall on his knees to pray, like a saint in a stained-glass window. Another had watched him 'throw himself at the foot of a crucifix' on receiving the famous telegram. A third, an American still greedier of sensation, transferred this scene to the Dominican monastery itself (instead of the guest-house) so that the setting should be more grand and those present more numerous. His account became an epic of suspense, with visual effects of mass movements of white-robed Fathers, thanksgiving and songs of praise! But even this record was beaten: one newspaper asserted that Father Pire had decided to enter a monastery at the age of three . . .

But it was not only the international newspapers which went slightly mad, ordinary people were affected as well. Among the several hundredweights of congratulatory messages, there were a number of complaints, notably from perpetual candidates for the Nobel award. One of them, writing on the wrapping from a block of chocolate, came out with all his dissatisfaction: 'If it hadn't been for you, I should have had the prize and been able to pay all my debts,' he remarked, severely.

Another wrote with sad resignation: 'So much the worse for 1958! I shall get it, I hope in 1959. After all, I am used to waiting, I have been a candidate nineteen years'.

Among the yet more extraordinary letters, one from a worthy English lady deserves to be quoted, in which she urged the Nobel Prizewinner to find her a husband: 'Although I am fifty-five, I still look like an unspoiled, young girl,' she went on artlessly.

But side by side with such harmless folly, how many touching letters there were, and how many generous gestures!

Mr. Otto Frank, father of little Anne Frank who died in Belsen, wrote:

I have read of your intention of building a village for Displaced Persons, and giving it the name of my daughter Anne. You can imagine how deeply moved I am by this idea, and, as I devote the royalties accruing from my daughter's diary to charitable and cultural projects, I am happy to send you the enclosed cheque for a thousand dollars, which I want you to dispose of as you wish.

In reply Father Pire said:

Thank you for your gift which will be converted to stones for building the Anne Frank Village. I have had a photograph of Anne pinned on the wall of my small office for some months now, and beyond her face I see all those who have suffered and who suffer now. I draw deep courage from it.

Father Pire's second day in Oslo ended in a heavy task, the writing of dedications in three hundred copies of the Diary of Anne Frank, *the gift of the publisher. These three hundred copies were to be sold at one hundred crowns apiece, that is 210,000 Belgian francs, the proceeds to be devoted to the European villages.*

Accordingly, the good father wrote his dedication, hour after hour: 'Cordial thanks, Father Dominique Pire'.

Meantime, the film men were busy, immersing the prize-winner in a heat bath, and making him very thirsty, so he drank lemonade in his refuge behind the piles of books, and then went back to his labours. Keeping a straight face, but with a hint of a wink, he told me that by evening, when he reached the two-hundredth dedication, he was astonished to find himself writing: 'Cordial Pire. Father Dominique thanks.'

CHAPTER FIFTEEN

———————————— ◆ ————————————

A Nobel Prize is not the End

AT LAST *the great day, when simplicity, generosity, and kindness, the three snow-white flowers of Norway, were to flower once more in that beautiful ceremony! Anywhere else, such an assembly would have been stiffly formal, with fan-fares and precisely ordered processions. In the course of my life, I have watched many displays glorifying Peace, for which the programmes noted that 'the Army will be taking part', but it could not be like that in Oslo, for everyone there combines proud-spirited patriotism with solid, civilian virtue . . .*

In this country the sovereign is guarded by sentries wearing hats with cock's feather plumes, who step out their hundred paces in front of a palace without railings, shouldering their guns in regulation fashion, not like a gun but like an axe. Soldier-lumberjacks; almost soldier-farmers.

Before where the sentries stand, little children, with cheeks and lips like glacé cherries, come and haul their toboggans. For King Olaf's home dominates the town, and the vista before it, lined on both sides by fine trees, provides a splendid icy slope which is not solely reserved for royal use!

Such simple goodness of heart is only found in the North: a palace with an approach just made for little children's toboggans. What an unusually rare pleasure it is to see democracy beginning with the nestlings!

I was waiting until it was time to go into the University Aula where, in the presence of the King, the Nobel Committee of the Norwegian Parliament would present the Peace Prize to Father Pire. The sky was blue, but the temperature was freezing at seven degrees below zero. I took refuge in one of Oslo's little tea-rooms, the Frascati, opposite the National Theatre and a favourite haunt of Norwegian ladies. From eleven o'clock onwards they chatter away, not over a cup of tea, but over huge and delicious sandwiches of sugared herring, smoked pork, or garnished with giant shrimps, plump as the Little Mermaid, which melt in the mouth in a dream of mayonnaise.

A gentle pianist tinkled through sad waltzes, and the frosted Christmas tree set on the piano caught up the sounds, transformed them to light and movement and glittered in triple time.

And was I now far away from the Nobel Prize and the official ceremonies? Not at all. The door opened and Dignity entered, in the person of a minister and one of the Nobel Committee. Both decorously selected their sandwiches and a quiet corner. You would never see such a thing in Brussels: it would be unthinkable, for example, to see a senator sharing a snack with the Minister of Justice, in a self-service bar in the centre of the city before some solemn occasion.

It was time now to go through the park, for the ceremony began at half-past one. Through the window I could see the white lawns and statues: Ibsen dreamed away on his plinth, wearing a snowy wig and buttoned into his fine bronze topcoat.

In the distance was the Greek portico of the University, the red carpet, and the crowd in their snow-boots. Encased in thick wool or hugged in their furs, they were awaiting the arrival of the King and the bigwigs.

It was time to find a place.

Many people had already gathered in the great white-

marble hall, with its symbolic frescoes in slightly acid colour tones. Conspicuous among members of the Diplomatic Corps were Monsieur du Bois, Belgian Ambassador to Oslo, and Mr. Kildal, Norwegian Ambassador to Brussels. It was a great day for both of them, but they each tried to hide their emotion in their own way: the Belgian by an exquisite politeness and the Norwegian by making himself as small as possible in a small corner.

Everything was in place: the rostrum with its gilded cornices, the red carnations beside the microphones, and the weighty gold medal and diploma of the Peace Prize lying on a table inside green morocco cases, decorated with white birds flying over a red and green landscape. Everything was very modern in style.

And now, here came the King and Princess Astrid, who had chosen her dress to match the warm colour of the carnations.

The assembly welcomed the sovereign with a wonderful silence, in which one could sense a deep friendliness, and then, high above in the musicians' gallery the stoic tempest of Beethoven's Coriolanus overture rang out. In the front row, Father Pire sat with closed eyes, collecting his thoughts.

Silence fell once more and Mr. Gunnar Jahn, President of the Nobel Committee, rose to speak. An elderly man, with a face rather like Churchill's, he walked up to the rostrum, buttoning his dinner jacket as he came, and in a faint but assured voice gave an excellent address, telling the story of the prizewinner's work, and giving an account of the chief events of his life. Among his notable comments were:

If one were to estimate the importance of Father Pire's work by the number of refugees he has rescued, some would say that the total did not amount to very much. But this is not a case to be judged by statistics. Far more important is the spirit which inspired Father Pire's work, and which he has sown abroad in the hearts of men. We may hope that the future will see it germinate in the form of disinterested endeavour for the cause of those of our fellows who are plunged in distress.

And this:

Father Pire's work for the refugees was undertaken to heal the wounds of war, but he looks much further than that and, as he has himself said, our aim should be to build a bridge of light and loving-kindness across the waves of colonialism and racial hatreds. And, further yet, to cultivate actively the development of a spirit of brotherhood among men, nations, and races. Alfred Nobel voiced the same thought in his will, when he said that the Prize for Peace should be awarded to the man who had toiled the hardest and most effectively for brotherhood among the peoples. That is why the Nobel Committee is pleased and honoured to present the prize for 1958 to the Reverend Father Dominique Pire.

The King, the Princess, and the whole audience rose to their feet. Called to the platform, Father Pire received the great golden medal, which shows on the reverse three men with their arms linked in friendship, their hands on each other's shoulders. His white robe reflected the glare of the flashlights, and he stood like a gleaming candle, hesitant and his eyes blurred by tears. Later he would say it was just the dazzle of the lamps that affected him.

The Belgian Ambassador coughed gravely, and his wife openly wept into her handkerchief. The Norwegian Ambassador to Brussels bowed his head in an attempt to hide his tears, and the situation was no better by the King's side: Princess Astrid was wiping her beautiful eyes.

Then Father Pire gave a speech of thanks, and when he ceased speaking he was answered by a storm of applause. Then the orchestra launched to the four corners of the hall Handel's Allegro, *an anthem of joy.*

It was the crowning moment of ten years of devoted

effort, not in the service of an abstract idea of Humanity, so much grey water which runs away between your fingers impossible to grasp, but of Man, the possessor of a heart and a body, suffering in the flesh and with a deadened or troubled soul.

The rules of the Nobel Foundation stipulate that each holder of the Nobel Peace Prize must deliver a lecture in Oslo within a year of the day on which he received the award. Father Pire didn't wait for the year to go by, nor a month, nor even a week. He gave his address on the very day after the presentation in the great hall of the Nobel Institute, itself an austerely magnificent palace built in the style of the nineteenth century, that age of the benevolent and splendid middle-class.

From the yellow vaulted ceiling of the great Hall of Honour, with its flights of the white doves dear to Peace, hung enormous crystal chandeliers. The speaker's rostrum was set in a kind of alcove hung with gold brocade.

Once more the beautiful white Dominican habit stepped towards a rostrum before a northern audience. This evening Father Pire's voice was stronger and more vibrantly convincing than ever. He was delivering neither a sermon nor a lecture, but giving voice to conscience in a militant appeal for human brotherhood:

'Men build too many walls and not enough bridges.'

Father Pire used these words of Newton as his opening.

I don't listen to the pessimists who say that all the Nobel Prizes have never done anything to prevent outbreaks of violence, he cried. I believe that the world does make spiritual progress, slow maybe, but sure—even if it is a matter of making two steps back for every three we go forward, it is still that third step that really counts.

212

This idea is clearly brought out in a message someone sent me :

'At first I said to myself : what he is doing is admirable, of course, but even if he does succeed in establishing ten or even twenty Old People's Homes, he is only saving a fraction of the Hard Core. But you have held firm and the efficacy of your work has increased by geometric progression. The moment will come when you will be able to resolve the complete problem, or at least have the final solution in sight. You are the living proof that it is here, and here only, that the real answer lies : to work with all one's heart and soul in the direction, however modest it may seem, that Providence suggests, and never to allow oneself to tire. An initial act of loving-kindness which seems at first to benefit only a few unknown people, ends by having world repercussions, and by becoming a means of international solidarity.'

And he went on:

People who think that I imagine the tragedy of the Displaced Persons comprises all the world's problem of suffering, are wrong. When I help a few European refugees, I see beyond them to all the refugees of Europe whom I am unable to help, and beyond these again to the refugees of the world.

And on the other side of the flood of refugees I see innumerable crowds of the afflicted : the hungry, the homeless, the imprisoned, and so on.

We can only remain humbly what God has made us and carry out the tasks He has appointed. My task is to continue to plough my little furrow in the field of Displaced Persons, in a spirit of love and patience, and exercising initiative, tenacity, and a realist assessment of what can be done. But though we must work each at our own task, we must not do so in isolation, but spreading peace wherever we are.

However deep our differences may seem to be, they are really only superficial, and that which divides us is of infinitesimal importance as compared with what we have in common. The best way for us to live in peace, to exist in mutual respect and love, is to fix our eyes on this common denominator, our shared humanity—a splendid phrase! Let us then learn again and again to see everyone, even though utterly different from us in his ideas, his social position, his outlook, or his beliefs as a brother human being. Let us learn again and again to put our fellow man at his true worth—which is infinite.

Deeply moved, Father Pire went on softly:

The happiness I feel at this moment is not merely pleasure in the award. I am no aged admiral receiving the last and finest decoration of my life. Mine is a deep, inward joy, a joy of the spirit, as if I were a mountaineer suddenly catching sight in the midst of his climb of a route which will lead him still higher.

The Nobel Peace Prize is not the final goal, only a beginning, and it puts an immense responsibility upon me.

Give me your help, dear friends, and enable me in that way to extend the scope of my efforts. Let us widen the road of brotherly understanding together!

Let us join in relieving the suffering of mankind.

CHAPTER SIXTEEN

The Heart Open to the World

I HAD TRAVERSED *the glass-walled corridor, the odd, sloping passageway which was so slippery that they had had to put down rubber floor-covering, and reached the fifteen narrow steps at the end.*

Father Pire was waiting for me in the doorway of the garret at the top, which was grandly referred to by his secretaries as 'The Office', and which he preferred to call his 'glory-hole'. He sat down at his table, or rather, as much of it as the Nobel Prize had left him for himself. After the award, as before, he remained the richest Poor Man in the world. It was only kindnesses to others, and their gratitude and friendship, that he had made a practice of hoarding.

I had come to find an end to this book, an unavailing quest, since the life of this man is symbolic of an eternal will: the awkwardly slow, but tireless, groping of Humanity towards good. Some pages should be left blank after the last chapter.

He did me the honours of his retreat. Sitting at his desk surrounded by little tables loaded with papers and by chests full of files, he was writing on a blotting-pad bound in a horrible green plastic cover. On the table there was a pot of tulips to his left, and a bunch of lilies of the valley and forget-me-nots to his right.

Relics of St. George's Day! he said.

On the right, facing visitors, was a map showing the world in two hemispheres. Why? I asked him.

Because I am world-minded!

For the same reason, there was another world map on the wall, which he had bought in Rome in 1932. The emblem of a plump heart, pierced with a window, had been stuck on it, the emblem of the 'Heart Open to the World'.

Alongside were stuck some Belgian stamps bearing the same device, for Belgium had commemorated the Nobel Peace Prize by offering Father Pire the money accruing from a special postal issue.

The two windows opening on to the courtyard could only be opened half way, and had to be wedged in position by matchboxes, because a forest of cacti was growing in front of them. Father Pire, himself the incarnation of gentleness, has a weakness for these bristly plants which only reward his care of them by pricks and scratches. Each little monster has a story attached to it. This one was given him by his mother, that has exceptional ear-like growths, and the one over there was brought back from Corsica in a suitcase. Yet another was surreptitiously detached from the wall of an old cemetery in the South of France, and the one at the end, a very rare specimen, is made of marzipan.

My eyes made a slow inventory of these and other trifles, each one the record of a friendship:

Photographs: one of the village of Bregenz, one of Anne Frank as a little girl (sent by her father), and one of a little nine-year-old girl, Francoise, whom he had seen die. An embroidered heart, sent by a little girl named Bernadette, and a terra-cotta hare, rather like a kangaroo. A snap of Father Pire and the King of Norway. A doll in national cos-

tume. A glass ash-tray engraved with the words: 'Everything comes to him who waits.' A photograph of Nansen, and a very bad portrait in oils of Dr. Schweitzer, which he kept because it was, like the rest, a token of friendship. A Belgian doctor, the father of six children, had diligently painted it and braved four customs posts, gravely imperilling his peace of mind, in order to present it to Father Pire on the day he laid the foundation stone of the Schweitzer Village at Spiesen. Following which, Father Pire was tortured by four customs posts, in the opposite direction, in the process of getting the picture back into Belgium.

A statuette of Our Lady of the Maquis, the Virgin of the Flight into Egypt. A certificate as an intelligence agent, signed Montgomery. A photo of Father Pire chatting with a gorgeously dressed Orthodox priest, taken at Hamburg.

On a shelf were official gifts: a pewter jug commemorating the tenth anniversary of the Aid for Displaced Persons organisation, a wooden dish given by the Mayor of Spiesen, plates painted with the arms of the European Villages, a Council of Europe pennon, and then a pine-cone picked up in Austria, and photos of Gandhi, Schweitzer, Nansen, and Anne Frank.

A pipe, the humorous offering of the Norwegian Ambassador, for Father Pire isn't a smoker. A penguin carved in sperm-whale ivory, a sponge penguin, a statuette of St. Joseph, the gold braclet belonging to the girl from Antwerp who had slipped it into Father Pire's hand 'for the poor' after hearing him lecture, an ivy plant, and a map of the Catholic and Protestant dioceses of Germany.

You can tell from these where I've been and the people I have talked to.

Behind a green curtain: the Peace Prize medal and diploma and a bottle of brandy that would never be uncorked;

217

*a radiogramophone that he had no time to listen to, and a
felt fishing cap that he would never wear. Lastly, on his
desk, a medal given by the Huy communal council, made
up at that periods of socialists and liberals.*

*And on the blank wall space a portrait of St. Nicolas of
Flue.*

Who is this saint, Father? I said.

A really extraordinary character! He had thirteen children and became a hermit.

Now, come along with me . . .

*We left the office and climbed a veritable bird-cage ladder.
Father Pire pushed open a door, and by some miracle we
found ourselves in a garden instead of an attic. The house
backs on to a spur of the steep hillside, which forms a terrace
at roof level, and there were tulips, rose bushes, turf, a
bench, and arbour, and sunshine. In the distance one could
see the hills of the Meuse.*

*Pacing up and down this rocky poop-deck, he went on
giving me his message.*

I have seen the suffering of the D.P.s and have tried to
relieve it, but through familiarising myself with it, I have
ended by understanding how this misery at Europe's heart
ought to draw all the people of Europe together in finding a
remedy.

Distress forms a pivot, the hub of a wheel, the throbbing
centre of my Europe of the Heart which isn't a territory,
or a military, economic, or political region, but a human
Europe, a Europe set in brotherhood. How can we build it?

Many men have attempted to do it by means of congresses
and conferences, but at these, though much is said of
Europe, little is done. During the Brussels World Exhibition

in 1958, twenty congresses a week assembled, most of them European: there were the European Congresses of Pastry-cooks, Plumbers, Multicopyists, Bridge-Players, and Anglers.

I even spoke myself in Strasbourg to a Congress of Five Thousand Accordionists. That's a splendid idea the Europe of the Accordion! But isn't there a far greater unifying force in the relief of suffering by a brotherly coalition?

But, before a river can be born, a spring must exist . . .

And what is that spring, Father?

Work for an unselfish end carried out together, and what better rallying point or meeting-place could there be than the common ground of suffering? The Hard Core is the iron soul around which the substance of the Europe of the Heart will form.

Oh, I don't visualise this union as a vast mass embrace, with two hundred million Europeans flinging their arms round one another's necks! We must be practical.

But men of goodwill everywhere must draw together to accomplish something together. I have seen it happen in Belgium: both socialist workmen and Freemasons have given me, a Catholic priest, money for my European Villages. In France Protestant parishes have done the same. Each has come forward, not in support of his own party, nation, or religion, but for others, and this is how I see Europe of the Heart. It tingles with life and advances along all sorts of byways.

Of course, the refugees are not guinea-pigs in an experiment in European brotherhood. Help to them and the preservation of their human dignity come before all.

How far does this Europe of the Heart extend?

To the farthest bounds of Siberia. I have no time to waste

on anti-Communism and am bound by no frontiers. I am not 'anti-' anything, but always 'pro-' something—'pro-human', in fact.

The only common denominator is our shared humanity.

I fight against barriers, prejudices, stereotyped social ideas. They correspond to certain realities, but are mainly comfortable cushions for our minds and hearts.

People say there is a quixotic element in my crusade, and I will not quarrel with their ironic criticism. Don Quixote was alone, but splendidly so, in his pursuit of the absolute. But I divine, breathing in the realisation like a perfume, that God is for Unity and Satan for Division.

His stride lengthened under the stress of his emotion, and his white habit flew out and caught on the rose bushes.

So your Europe of the Heart, I said, goes as far as Siberia's boundaries. What about the lands beyond?

His eyes were unseeing, turned inward on his thoughts, as he replied:

Don't think that the idea of 'beyond' hasn't haunted me for years! That is why I have just decided to found an even greater work, based on universal humanity—The Heart Open to the World.

Oh, I shall not desert my first children : the D.P.s.

But offers and appeals reach me from all over the world, and it is impossible for me to be deaf to any cry of affliction, however far off it may be.

People write to me : they want to work for me, campaign for me, help to build, lend their aid. Others appeal to me : the hopeless, the mad, the poor, the misfits, the released prisoners, the lonely men and women, and those who want to adopt orphans.

They draw my attention to wholesale distresses, and I

want to respond to this world outcry without being crushed by the aligned World Powers.

Shall I try to help the refugees of Pakistan ?

Shall I knock on the Iron Curtain to ask Poland to let me in ? What I want to make clear is that the Nobel Peace Prize ignores all barriers, just as does Peace itself.

Father, those barriers are high.

They don't reach to the sky. I must try. I haven't had a single hour's peace of mind since the Nobel prize.

What is God's will in planting in me this disquiet ? It is a mystery . . . Does He wish me to remain entirely devoted to work for D.P.s alone, or is there something else ?

Perhaps you will receive a message?

No, said Father Pire slowly. God does not give direct messages, he just gives a hint, a whisper . . .

He writes indirectly. though his meaning is clear if we read between the lines.

Someone called to us. The evening post had come. Father Pire read the letters through, sad-faced, then suddenly his features relaxed, and he held out a sheet of paper with almost an air of tenderness.

A little girl in a camp in Austria had written:

Dear Father,
    We have your letter and your parcel, your kind words and the sugar. They made us apricot jam and happiness. Thank you for both.

What will you do to help?

Here is the address:

R.P. Dominique Pire,

Aide aux Personnes Deplacées,

35 rue du Marché,

Huy, Belgium.